Praise for *Parenting the Children of Now*

"*Parenting the Children of Now* is a treasure hunt for your wonder, passion, and authenticity as a person, and also as a parent. Losey presents an upfront and honest approach with a dose of humor, as well as heart wisdom. The easy-to-follow format with discussion, exercises for yourself, and ones to share with your children makes for easy reading and essential practices as you find your get-real self to parent the new generation."

    —Dr. Caron Goode, founder of The Academy for Coaching Parents, author of *Raising Intuitive Children* and *Kids Who See Ghosts*

"Don't wait. Read *Parenting the Children of Now* by Meg Blackburn Losey, NOW! This book is required reading for parents raising bright, aware, and sensitive children. Whether you are a teacher, minister, doctor, therapist, or a family member, [you can] benefit enormously from the profound insights, humor, compassion, and practical instructions Dr. Meg offers to help guide us through the magical, yet often challenging, years of growing up aware and, more often than not, invalidated."

    —Michael J. Tamura, internationally renowned spiritual teacher, visionary, healer, and award-winning author of *You Are the Answer: Discovering and Fulfilling Your Soul's Purpose*

"*Parenting the Children of Now* encourages outside of the box, honest living in parents that perceptive, intuitive children will feel in their core. It supports parents as they take a close look at their emotional well-being so that they can be fully present and congruent in their parenting. This book will support you in the task of weeding out life's little untruths, making peace with the past, and being intentional in the now. All of this translates into more emotional skill and safety within the family that helps kids feel safe in expressing—and being—all of who they are born to be."

    —Catherine Crawford, LMFT, ATR, author of *The Highly Intuitive Child*

"I wish that when I was a young mother I could have had a book like this one to guide me—for my own sake, and for that of my kids. One thing's for certain, I will buy a copy of this book for each of my children, even though they are now in their forties and fifties—for them, their kids, and their grandkids yet to come. Dr. Meg Blackburn Losey sees what needs to be addressed—How are we going to have better kids if we don't have better parents? Who are you as a parent? Who is that child you have?— and climbs right into the subject with gusto, confronting every issue parents have with themselves. She holds firm on teaching ethics and honesty no matter what, and on listening to children and giving them love—lots of it. The larger view she takes on parenting is exceptional. Every parent and grandparent should have this book. I've never come across anything quite like it."

—P.M.H. Atwater, LHD, author of *Beyond the Indigo Children, The Big Book of Near-Death Experiences,* and *Future Memory*

"A huge thank you to Dr. Meg for celebrating these children. *Parenting the Children of Now* gives parents an awareness about their hang-ups (and fears) of how their children 'should' be and provides tools to change that kind of thinking within themselves. In doing so, each parent will begin to see the daily miracles that are present in these children. Dr. Meg shows us that when we let go of our fears about ourselves and our children, all of their gifts can become evident. Bravo!"

—Marilu Schmier, mother of Weston Schmier, featured in *The Children of Now* and *Parenting the Children of Now*

PARENTING
the CHILDREN
of NOW

Practicing Health, Spirit, and Awareness
to Transcend Generations

Meg Blackburn Losey, Ph.D.

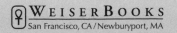
WEISERBOOKS
San Francisco, CA / Newburyport, MA

To David

First published in 2009 by
Red Wheel/Weiser, LLC
With offices at:
500 Third Street, Suite 230
San Francisco, CA 94107
www.redwheelweiser.com

ISBN: 978-1-57863-460-6
Library of Congress Cataloging-in-Publication Data available upon request.

Cover and interior design by Maija Tollefsen
Typeset in Sabon
Cover photograph © Karl Rosencrants/istockPhoto

Printed in the United States of America
TS
10 9 8 7 6 5 4 3 2 1

⊕ Text paper contains a minimum of 30% post-consumer-waste material.

Contents

Acknowledgments

There are always a gazillion people who have a hand in our life experience, who directly and inadvertently contribute to who we are. To each of you, too many to name, who have touched my heart and soul along the way, there are no words to express the perfection that we have shared and created together. This work and others are the synergy of us as a collective.

To all of the parents who wrote to me, stopped me in my tracks, and called me, this book is for you. Remember that your children aren't broken—we just have a lot to learn. I am grateful for your abiding interest in this ongoing subject. Keep asking your questions. Together we have learned an invaluable amount of new and exciting information about us, our children, consciousness, and the new evolution of humanity.

To Devra, my friend, my agent, and publicist who has believed in me from day one. You are a goddess in my heart! Thank you for being there 24/7 always with a smile and the energy to make your ideas and mine come alive.

Great Gratitude, with a capital G, to Jan and Red Wheel /Weiser Publishing for believing enough in me to take me on long term. We have great things to say together.

Posthumously to my most wonderful friend Van: I remain forever touched by your presence and I am still listening.

And finally, to the Children of Now. I hear you and I won't let you down.

Introduction

I can't count the number of parents who have written to me, filled with angst that they have been graced with one or more of the Children of Now. Many of these parents are nearly panicked, thinking that something is wrong with their kids. Because their children are so sensitive, astute in matters of life and heart, the children are often seen as abnormal, in need of, lacking, or just plain strange.

Some of them are! Such children are gifts to our world and, more to the point, to humanity. Great numbers of these kids have such deep powers of observation and intuitive feeling that they are often way ahead of us, and we don't know what to do with that.

The truth is that there isn't anything at all wrong with our kids. The problem lies with us. Society—and beyond. We turn a blind eye to the fact that humanity has evolved to a greater state of awareness and sensitivity. We, as a society, are so bound by the rules we have created that we have lost sight of what we are really doing. We have lost sight of the personal, of the experience of life. We refuse to bend, choosing to stay in our safe zones because they are predictable. We maintain the same school curriculums that were set in place over a hundred years ago. We are living by archaic systems, perceptions, and rules. It is time for change.

In every moment, being born into this world are children who are part of a fast-forward evolution of the consciousness of humanity. These kids are gifted in ways that we don't always understand. They are intuitive, wise beyond their years, sentient, feeling everything beyond their five senses with their entire bodies. They fidget; they move beyond the speed of light, never seeming to land until they finally fall asleep.

Many, many of these children, whom I call the Children of Now, are being diagnosed with ADD, ADHD, and bipolar disorders. They are being drugged so that they fit the expected norm of society and our school systems. They are carrying the stigma of dysfunction, and because of this, they are coming to believe that they are not good enough, broken, and in some cases, perhaps even undeserving of life. But there is nothing wrong with them.

Nothing.

At all.

Period.

The Children of Now exhibit expanded human awareness—the ability to think holographically. These children mentally store data as if their brains are compartmentalized and have intricate filing systems.

Many of the Children of Now come into our world remembering their origins, their existence before coming to earth. They remember talking to God, choosing their parents, and even their past lives.

And they are on a mission.

The Children of Now are here to help us remember who we are as human beings. We have forgotten that everyone is connected and that we all matter—significantly—no matter who we are, what color our skin is, what we believe, or even who our God is. The kids know that beyond our belief systems there is simple knowing. They know that it is impossible to understand everything and that the entirety of being is part of an expansive organism in which we are all not only related, but also connected.

The Children of Now often say things that are so profound it is as if they are messengers of God, as if they are wise sages reaching into the infinite and pulling out sentiments that rock us to our cores.

In spite of appearances and in spite of their wisdom and perceptions, these kids have real needs. They are being sabotaged by society and even their family systems due to simple ignorance. The Children of Now need our help. The problem is that, for the most part, we don't know how to help ourselves. We don't want to look at our own problems. We aren't even sure what those problems are. Our life issues, our pain, our disappointment, our grief, our confusion about how we fit in, and our past experiences are all balled up in a wad of feelings that work in our subconscious to drive our choices and inhibit our ability to fully embrace life. We sabotage our experiences so that they reflect the belief that we really don't deserve or aren't good enough.

We must learn to clean up our acts. We must become what we mean and, within that becoming, learn to act as examples of excellence of humanity to our children.

This book isn't about the children. It is about us—we, the adults who were taught to do more, to try harder, to find our purpose in life. Unfortunately no one ever gave us a road map to those destinations or told us what it looked like when we succeeded in finding them.

We have the capability to move beyond our comfortable discomfort and into a place of wholeness, internal truth, and impeccability, first with ourselves and then with our children. They need us.

Children don't come with an instruction manual. How can we possibly know what to do and how to give them everything that they need emotionally, physically, mentally, and spiritually? The main reason that we have so many questions about how to raise our kids is that we haven't really learned about ourselves as human beings. We struggle with our own challenges as we move into adulthood, quickly forgetting what it was like when we were innocent and saw the world much differently.

In order for us to really get it as parents and caregivers, we must first become aware of our own stuff—our fears, our issues, those things that keep us from being completely free within ourselves—so that we can live life to its fullest. Once we are aware of our stuff, then we can take action to move past it. We all have stuff underlying everything we do. We make our decisions and react to life based upon our previous experiences and our subconscious beliefs and feelings, which perhaps we aren't even aware of.

What if we were able to come clean with ourselves? What if we were at complete ease in every aspect of our lives? Wouldn't that make a huge difference in how we approach what we teach our children directly and by example?

This book is about us. It describes a vastly different approach to raising our children than anything else to date. In order for us to be the kind of parents that we want to be, we must first be the kind of people we want to be—the people we think we are.

This is a handbook for becoming aware of our internal stuff, the illusions that keep us from stepping into our magnificence and passing our magnificence down to our children. It is about the kind of things that keep us stuck in our lives, believing that we are not perfect and that someone or everyone else is more knowledgeable, smarter, better looking, more compassionate, more *anything* than we are. It is my hope, my wish for you, that the words on these pages bring to the surface your issues from your very core, so that you can regurgitate them out of your psyche and make room for the kind of life you really want. Further, it is my intention to share with you the secrets of creating a greater life that will naturally spill into every aspect of your existence and into generations to come. It *is* possible.

Generationally we have lived from the perspective that we are damaged people who are far less than perfect. We have spent our lives trying to be what everyone else thinks we should be. Move over everyone. We are coming out of ourselves, and we are magnificent creatures!

If we cannot be healthy, functional adults with a terrific self-image and the ability to see our inner being from the perspective of honesty and clarity, how can we possibly think that we can raise a new generation of children who are infinitely more sensitive than we ever were and enable them to become the amazing people they have the potential to be?

What aspects of our subconscious or conscious behaviors will our children carry as part of their psyche, their inner being, as they grow into their future lives? What familial patterns will we bequeath to our children? Which of our fears will they take into their own being and thus cause them to be dysfunctional?

Who we are, how we act and interact with *everyone,* is what our children ultimately become. If we, as the caregivers of these amazing beings, do not become healthy, balanced people, we are doing a disservice to them, ourselves, and ultimately our future and our children's future.

As a whole, we adults have a huge number of issues that most of us are not aware of, can't admit to, or just don't know how to get past. We move through our challenges kicking and screaming and fighting the ultimate changes that will occur in spite of our resistance. We don't generally have healthy relationships because we don't know how. Or we are so mired in issues with our own parents that we subconsciously seek out and involve ourselves in relationships that have similar dynamics.

Many of us don't feel special or as if we even belong on the planet; we feel like home is really some nebulous memory from our distant past, and we can't remember how to get back there. We don't feel like we fit in with other people. We have lost our innocence and don't remember how to laugh because we are working so hard to be responsible. Caught in the loop of job, life, and home, we often miss the wonders that are around us in any given moment. We look to others to give us value and believe that they have more power than we do, and we become complacent, not standing up for what we know or believe. We inadvertently lie to ourselves on a regular basis in order to convince ourselves that our lives are exactly what we want or that we are stuck with what we have.

If we can't look at and face our own issues, how in the heck are we going to raise a new generation of the most gifted human beings that have graced the planet? Without change we will be passing down to our new generations the same patterns that we inherited from our predecessors.

This is a new time—life isn't like it was in previous generations. We are smarter, the world is faster, communications are beyond light speed, and our entire value systems are different. Do we really know what is important?

We don't know how to nurture ourselves. We don't know what we need.

Worse, we create families we don't know how to relate to. We love our children with all our hearts. We want our children to have the best of everything, and in the process of making that happen, we lose touch with them. We don't know how to communicate with our kids. We don't usually stop to really hear what they are saying. We don't notice when they are having a hard day because we are caught in our own, and so we teach them to deal with things by not dealing with them rather than to process their problems in a healthy way. Many of us spend, literally, only a couple to a few hours in direct relationship with our kids on any given day.

We are quite fortunate that we have a new and gifted generation of children who are wise beyond their years, who are intuitive to the core, who feel everything with their entire being, and who are sensitive enough to see things as they truly are. On the other hand, we are doing them a great disservice. We aren't honest with them because we aren't honest with ourselves, and they know this.

We see that our children are mature beyond their size and years, and so we force them to have more responsibility than they need or really want. What they need is for us to responsibly, and from a place of healthfulness of body, mind, and spirit, teach them how to live in our world with balance, grace, and ease. But first we have to learn how to do this ourselves.

This book is the handbook to life that we never got. It is a set of life skills that we can utilize to change our lives and our life experiences into a greater, fuller existence. This is unquestionably the kind of change that we will have to make if our children are going to get what they will have and carry their giftedness forward into generations to come. The Children of Now are not just our seed, the result of our family lineage. They are far beyond that. They are the guardians of humanity and planet earth. They are here to bring us around before it is too late.

If we don't change our ways, we will squash these kids into mundane oblivion. They are everything that we ever imagined, the totality of who we are in truth.

They are to be seen.

They are to be heard.

And so are we.

We are the ones who stand on the precipice of their successes. Are we going to throw them to the wolves or teach them to fly? If we aren't willing to take off into the unknown, how can we teach our children to be any different?

If we do not allow ourselves to become everything that we can, to remember who we are, then we do a disservice to ourselves and all humanity. We are everything that we seek. Never are we less than perfection, except by our own perceptions. What if we looked beyond those beliefs and hidden emotions and got down to the nitty-gritty truth?

So here is the question: Who are you and what do you want? I mean really. Most of us go about our lives with an idealistic version of what our life should look like, what the experience should be. And yet most of us don't have a clue why our lives aren't turning out to be what we thought they ought to be.

If we ask ourselves who we really are and what we truly want, most of us can't answer that question honestly or directly. That is because we are trying to fit into other people's molds and their expectations and ideals. Plus, we are conditioned from birth to believe that we are not perfect, that we must achieve a singular purpose in our lives, and that we have to do it all by a certain set of rules. So we struggle, day after day, with our dreams just outside of our grasp, with our insecurities and fears leading the way to certain and ultimate disaster. Believe me, I found out the hard way!

Over ten years ago I found myself in what a lot of people might call a dark night of the soul. I awoke on my friend's couch sobbing. To this day I don't know what I was crying about. It could have been any number of things that morning. Everything that I had perceived to be my life had fallen apart in a short two weeks. Life. Love. Work. All gone in a flash. I had opted for my friend's couch because home had become impossible. I was working out of my car because my partners had pushed me out of the very business that I had conceived, planned, and created. There was more, but suffice it to say that there was nothing left of life as I had known it.

As I lay there in a puddle of my tears, I knew that something was terribly wrong. I knew that if I was to survive all of the challenges that now loomed before me, I really needed to understand where I had gone wrong. As I took an honest look at my life and the relationships I had developed with others, in that moment that I realized that life had been one lie after another. Lies that I told myself. Lies I had accepted from others because I wanted something from them.

I realized that all of my successes had been one great big illusion, that they were successes based upon the values of others, not mine.

I had no idea who I was or what I really wanted. I began to consider each situation from the perspective of me. Not what anyone else said or did. *My* part of the play. *My* game. What *was* my part in all of this? What was I fighting so hard to save or to be? Why was so much conflict around me when my heart had true desire to experience life with peace and to its fullest potential? After all, I *am* a loving and gentle person.

Conflict was the last thing I desired. All I ever wanted was to be loved and accepted. But somehow it felt as if I were surrounded by sharks, and I was the only item on the menu! Why was it so hard? What was my part in this disaster I called my life?

As I considered all of these things and more, what I began to realize was that the life I had created was based upon what I thought *everyone else* wanted me to be. I was trying to be the star of someone else's play. What did *I* want? I had no idea. Who was I, *really?* Who knew? I was a lie to myself.

One thing I realized beyond a shadow of a doubt that fateful morning was that enough was enough. I got it. *I really got it.* I was done. No more lies. No more self-deception. No more trying to be what everyone else expected. From that moment forward, I decided, enough was enough. And as I did, I looked up and said to no one in particular, "Whoever I am, whatever this is, *I accept!*"

They say you get what you ask for, but I had no idea how true that could be. That morning was the beginning of a life that is pure magic. As humble as I was, as low as I had fallen, the only way to go was up. No more being a victim of my own doings.

The first thing that happened was that the difficulties began to melt away. I lost weight. My body began to reflect who I really was. The people with whom I had been involved slunk into my past, and new people began to show up. Honest, considerate, caring people. People who were open to the possibilities of greater reality. Positive people who lived from their hearts and interacted with sincerity and without a self-agenda. They didn't want anything from me.

Each day I practiced telling the truth to myself and others, and honestly at first that was one of the scariest things I had ever done. I felt raw and exposed, but my conviction to be nothing less than the true me won, time after time, day after day. And ultimately telling the truth became easier.

As I learned to be authentic, my intuitive gifts unfolded, and I realized that there was much, much more to being alive than I had ever imagined. I began to realize the power of the moment and, even more important, the power of myself. I realized that life isn't so hard once we get the hang of it, but that we have to live it from a very simple set of instructions. I learned that creating the kind of experience that I wanted in life was as easy as believing it, and that worrying was nothing more than fear of "what ifs" that didn't even exist.

I began to unfold, celebrating myself as a beautiful human being who had no stories to cover up, no lies to tell, but was just an authentic person on a mission to herself. As each day became easier, it also became more magical, and I realized that I was onto something.

I was not just at ease—I was *free*. I was present with myself for the first time in my life, and I actually liked me. It seemed that there was no end to the realities I could create from my new life perspective. I learned that anything was as easy as imagining it. All I had to do was think something, and it became instant reality. If there was something that I wanted to know or understand, someone I had never met before showed up in my living room with the answers. I became the queen of synchronicities!

I learned to laugh at myself, to express my inner passions, emotions, even my fears—all without feeling unsafe. The little kid in me was no longer afraid to come out and play. People began to notice great changes in me and wanted to know what I was doing. I tried to tell them, but the enormity of life change was so new to me that I didn't really have words. Sometimes there just aren't any.

One day a man came to my home and asked me to speak at his conference. Someone had told him about me, and he thought I had a lot to offer. Before that moment I hadn't even considered such an idea. I was at once elated and terrified. Who would believe *me*? Why would anyone want to hear *my* experiences? And yet something deep inside of me screamed at me to share what I had learned.

The weekend of the conference, I showed up and shuffled my feet the entire time that I told my story. I really thought everyone would leave.

I was far from wrong. No one walked out on me; in fact, when my allotted time was over, no one even moved. They were riveted in their seats, wanting more. Wow. Wow.

That lecture was the beginning of an entirely new and different life path for me. That weekend I met numerous people, and each became an important facet of my life. I grew to love every one of them dearly. It was as if a family of souls had traveled forever and come to rest together in one place in one moment in time.

Some became business associates over time, and some became great friends.

Since that fateful weekend, I have continued to follow each synchronicity that comes my way, without a thought or concern. I have learned a new definition of faith. I have learned the true meaning of letting go. And I have learned to love myself.

For over ten years now I have worked with individuals, families, and groups in the capacity of healer, counselor, teacher, and spiritual advisor. I have traveled around the world as a lecturer, keynote speaker, and instructor, teaching countless people how to create the kind of lives that they want.

Throughout my appearances and classes, no matter where I was or who was in the audience, the same issues came up over and over again. Nearly everyone had the same burning questions, and all of them were ones that I had faced in my own quest for a greater life.

As I listened to each question, each plea for understanding, I felt people's great need for more than our world seems to offer. None of who we are or what we are capable of has anything to do with a particular belief system. The real secret is that *there is no secret.* Everything is right here, inside of us, waiting for us to realize that we already have everything we need to be, have, or experience— *whatever we want.* There is magic inside of each and every one of us. We can create anything that we want anywhere, anytime, if only we have the right set of tools and the realization that we are subject to no one else's ideas or ideals, but our own.

Innately, our children know all of this. But we teach them to forget, and this is a travesty to our now and our future.

I want to share these tools with you. You have gifts that you haven't even considered. Why not discover who you really are and what you really want, and begin to create your life intentionally, creating from moment to moment the very kind of life that you want?

It is time to stop stumbling through life—"living by accident," I call it. The bottom line is that life is a choice. My question to you is, *who is doing your choosing?*

Parenting the Children of Now is about finding our power inside and bringing that power from the inside out. It is about taking that power into the creative process of our very lives, so that we can find ourselves fulfilled and overflowing with abundance. This book is about how—when we drop our pretenses and our perceptions of control, shed our fears, and embrace who we are—not only our creative gifts blossom, but we can also create a perfect life right here on earth.

Life is a series of choices, moment to moment. In each of those moments are signposts, clues, and even synchronicities that bring us closer to our intended goals. If we are living in fear, if we are bound by uncertainties, if we are worried about what has already happened or what is next, we are missing the boat. *Parenting the Children of Now* will teach you how to shed those fears, uncertainties, and perceptions of being less than, and bring you clearly onto a path of universal cocreation.

This is a new beginning for you. It is an opportunity for you to change your consciousness from never ending questions to a totality of answers.

Parenting the Children of Now will not only bring you self-empowerment, but will also empower your children. This is not just another self-help book. It is a book with an attitude. In it, you will find no-nonsense truth that may hit you square between the eyes or straight in the heart. So be it. If you don't want change in any aspect of your life, please, put this book down now and go do something else.

We can indefinitely or forever skirt around our issues, or we can quit deluding ourselves and get to it. *Parenting the Children of Now* is a journey through self, an embracing of the infinite possibilities that are available to us as human beings and infinite souls.

This is not a book of advice, but a true suite of instructions that bring about the possibilities inside of each of us. It is a set of tools that, if utilized, brings about true personal freedom. These truths, learned and lived, will reflect from us to the Children of Now the kind of world that they already know exists.

Societal changes usually begin within the heart of one person who has an idea that is timely and greater in scope than anything ever experienced in the perceptions of that society. What if, in your heart, you embraced the idea of being a whole, healthy being and passed that idea on to your children and the children of others?

Life is a gift and so are we. Why not get past the wrappings and into the heart of it? Change in our selves promises healthy perspectives and healthy life skills for our children. From there, there are no limits to what we and our new generations will create together and what we will leave for future generations.

1

GET REAL: ACCEPT YOURSELF

Who am I really? I haven't a clue!

Most of us don't have a clue who we are or what we really want. We have lived to please everyone else for so long that we are not often even aware that we want something different.

How did we get so far off track?

Like our children, we want to be accepted by others, to fit in, to be noticed, or recognized. Because of this desire, we have allowed ourselves to be conditioned by others to accept less in our lives, to accept untruths from others, and to generally disregard our own dreams, desires, opinions, and even the experiences that we want in our lives. No more!

One of the most detracting aspects of our self-perception and how we function in our lives is what we believe about ourselves. Our self-perceptions cause us to respond to every situation in life from that point of view. If we do not believe ourselves to be whole and perfect, then we are operating from the standpoint of imperfection, self-defense, negative self-image, and need.

When we operate from this aspect of self-perception, we show our children that they aren't perfect either. We teach them to defend themselves against the views and actions of others when, honestly, neither of these things has anything to do with them. People make choices. They have opinions. And those choices and opinions are theirs—not ours, not our kids'.

Because they are so sensitive, the Children of Now quickly gain a poor self-image. On top of that, they feel everything that we do and understand even what we don't. And by our example, we show them it is normal and acceptable to ignore our inner issues and dysfunctional behaviors that result from doing so. The children already feel different, as if they don't fit, and then, just like we learned to do, they learn to stuff away those feelings and to act as if nothing is wrong.

Because they have no coping skills to deal with their sensitivities in relation to the stark aspects of life, many of the children will become cosmically ill, as I call it. They come up with fevers, seizures, and illnesses that can't be defined by allopathic medicine, as well as erratic behaviors and emotional problems. Some of them even become self-destructive, using drugs, abusing alcohol, and even engaging in self-mutilation or, worse, attempting suicide as they get older.

How can we be better examples of healthy beings for our kids? First of all, we must learn to see ourselves as whole and perfect and stop believing that we are anything else.

Generationally speaking, most of today's adults come from backgrounds that were filled with the expectations of parents and other caregivers. In most cases, our parents and caregivers did their very best to give us what they thought we needed. They gave us the life tools that they had, but much of the time, their life toolbox was missing some very basic skills. They were heavily influenced by a generation that never questioned authority, period. The rules were followed, even when those rules were in the best interest of some, but not others. Our predecessors lived in a simple time when it occurred to very few that there could be more to life than there was.

In most of our families, we were told that we should do more, try harder, find our singular purpose in life, and be the best at it. Unfortunately, we weren't ever told what life would look like when we got there. We were given a road map with lots of traffic rules, but no destinations.

Further, we were expected to behave in certain ways, to follow the social norms of the times, and God forbid we should have expressed our real feelings. If we did, we were reprimanded or punished just for telling the truth. We were told that we weren't being good girls or boys. We weren't encouraged to talk about things that hurt us. On the contrary, we were told to be quiet, or we were ignored altogether. So we learned to bury that pain.

If someone we encountered was different somehow or didn't fit the social norm, we were taught to shun them. We were basically taught that if they weren't like us, they were weird or simply not acceptable. Judgment became prevalent in our lives.

Many of our religions taught us that we had to be subservient, that we were blemished by the sins of man, which set us against a powerful God who would strike us down if we did not obey. We were taught that we were weak beings who must strive to atone for our sins—basically that we were sinners from the word go.

This writer actually remembers as a small child having to go to confession weekly at school to report my sins to the parish priest. Confession was mandatory every Friday morning. I remember asking one of the nuns if, gee, I didn't have any sins, would I have to go to confession? She said that everyone sinned and that I absolutely must go. So I went, fearing a vengeful God. I literally had to make up sins when I went. And therefore I became the sinner that I hadn't been before. Kneeling on the stone dais, doing penance for sins I hadn't really committed, seemed like a paradox even then. I would justify the punishment because I had lied to the priest about my sins. So there I was, praying like crazy to atone for sins I would not have committed had I not been forced to participate in confessing sins I never had done. Instead of teaching me how to be honest, my religion taught me how to lie even when the situation was supposedly a blessed sacrament!

As we were subtly conditioned to "acceptable" behaviors, slowly and steadily our sense of self became confused and even buried. We learned not to show our feelings because doing so was easier than handling the conflict we might face if we did. We learned early on to defend ourselves by telling little white lies or even bigger ones to those around us.

Similarly, we learned to lie to ourselves about how things were going. After all, we wanted to believe that we were good people, achieving all that was expected of us! Over time, being dishonest with ourselves and others became a habit, and somewhere in all of those little lies we lost touch with who we really were.

In every direction of our development we were undermined. Our experience was a constant paradox. We felt damned if we did what we were told and followed the rules because we were not feeling free to be ourselves, and damned if we didn't because our behavior was considered unacceptable. Naturally, we began to look to our peers to tell us how we fit in, how we were doing, and whether or not we were right or wrong. We began to look externally for approval and validation of most everything we did or said. Some of us would have done nearly anything to feel as if we belonged or to be accepted.

But here is the kicker: everyone we asked could only answer us from *their* frame of reference. The set of life tools and discernment that they had wasn't exactly that full either. So it was like the blind leading the blind.

Because of this situation, many of us find ourselves floundering, lost, misdirected, and not knowing who we are or what we want. We strive to please people who developed with similar maps to ours, and the result isn't always a pretty picture. Our children see our behaviors and begin to subconsciously mimic them.

Still, we look to others to fill our perceived emptiness, to validate us, or to offer their approval. By perception, we give our power away, thinking that we never had any power anyway. We have come to see ourselves as alone in the world, separate from everyone and everything. We imagine that the experiences we have couldn't possibly be understood by anyone else. And in our separateness grows our deep and often painful sense of aloneness. From our feelings of isolation come self-defensive behaviors that cause us the very problems we want to avoid, and our situations are compounded with disappointment after disappointment.

The Truth May Hurt, but at Least It's Mine!

The only way to get real is to tell the truth, first to ourselves and then to others. As we close ourselves off, defining our experiences by how deep our pain was or how disappointed we were, wishing and hoping for the excellent experiences we have had to linger longer, we become unsure what we want. We aren't even sure we deserve it because we can't see our value, so we have this deep sense of being unfulfilled. If we don't know how to be happy, how can we teach our children to be happy?

We begin to develop a sense that we should be doing something else with our lives or that something greater is just around the corner, but we don't know how to get from here to there.

This brings me back to my original questions. Who are you really? Do you know? Do you remember? What *do* you want in life?

The greatest, most powerful words that anyone can ever say about their life are "I accept."

"I accept" means embracing yourself just as you are, without the perceived need to be anything but the true you and without the need to please anyone else.

If you really want things to change, accept *you* unconditionally. Whoever you are, whatever that looks like—just accept you as you. No strings, no pretenses, no preconceptions, no judgment. Just be willing to experience yourself undiluted by everyone else's opinions. Of course, you can't just *think* it and make it so. Self-acceptance is a way of life. It is about staying true to *you*, no matter what.

The truth is that in every given moment we have lived, we have done the best that we could. There are no mistakes, only opportunities to learn, change, grow—or not.

The first step to realizing who we are is to stop the untruths we tell ourselves as well as others. Untruths begin when, based upon our experiences and interactions with others, we are uncomfortable inside of ourselves. Our body signals to us that we are in a danger zone, and we react. Unfortunately, perhaps we haven't yet found the courage to state our truth in the moment, and we want everything to be easy with others. So we react often at our own expense.

Mentally we begin to toss things around in our brains like a washing machine on a spin cycle. The information never resolves because it is moving in a repetitive circle. Ultimately our brain will make leaps and assumptions in order to find some sort of logic in our experiences. And that logic is often far from the truth.

We don't realize that mentality or cyclic thinking will never, ever, lead us to truth. Mental resolution is only an illusion to satisfy the ego.

We tell ourselves any number of untruths. We might tell ourselves that even though someone else isn't treating us right, they don't mean it. We might tell ourselves that we are loved and wanted by someone who doesn't give us the first indication that is so. We might tell ourselves that we communicate brilliantly with our kids when we really don't understand what they need or how they feel at all. We might tell ourselves that our significant other would never fool around on us when, in fact, there is blatant evidence that they would (or are). We might tell ourselves that we are doing a good job when, in fact, we are slacking off because we really hate our job. We might tell ourselves that we are great parents when we barely spend any time at all with our children. We might tell ourselves that we will spend all weekend with our children while knowing deep down that finishing our project at work is our priority. We might tell ourselves most anything if it makes things seem to fit our lives or makes us more comfortable with our experiences. And ultimately we begin to feel unsettled, unhappy, and even sick.

With each self-deception, we fall farther and farther away from knowing who we are.

If we are to know what we want, even what we need, we must be able to *recognize* those wants and needs.

It is time to stop pretending that everything is just fine. It is time to let go of the illusion that we are something that we are not, and to find out just who is hiding behind all of the distractions that our lies have created. When we are in truth with ourselves, our children learn how to be in truth with themselves as well.

If what we feel inside is equal to what we feel on the outside, then we are in good shape, balanced, and honest with ourselves. When we are not being honest with ourselves, our body begins to give us signals. One of the first things that happens is that we hold our breath. We get tension in our chest, shoulders, or neck, or we get that lurching feeling inside our chest, as if a herd of elephants just stampeded across our equilibrium. Mood shifts can be another sign that we are not really comfortable with what is going on.

When our bodies signal us that we are out of truth, we need to start paying attention. Stop. Right then. Take a step back, and ask yourself to what is your body reacting. Catch it in the now. What was your last thought? What was it about? Was it really the truth, or did you just tell yourself that so that you would feel better?

Listen. What do you hear? What do you hear inside of *you? What is your body saying to you?* Find the untruth and tell yourself the *real* truth, even if it means that things are not going to be the same anymore. Let's face it; if life were *that good,* you sure wouldn't be feeling discomfort!

Bonus Exercise: Learning to Accept You

Let's take just a few minutes to make a point here. Close your eyes and think about how perfect you are. Uh oh. Do you see how your objections start right away? You might be thinking, "I am not pretty. I am not strong. I am not smart enough. I . . ." Well, you get the point.

So let's start again. Close your eyes. Direct your attention into the center of your chest, to that place where you feel love at its fullest. That feeling, that love, is the truth of who you are, no matter what is happening or how you see things. So let's start here. As you direct your attention into the very core of your heart, breathe in, slowly and intentionally.

As you breathe in, say to yourself something like "I accept my perfection. Whoever I am, whatever that looks like, I accept." Now breathe out, knowing that all negative thoughts are leaving you with your breath as you exhale.

Bonus Exercise with Your Child

It doesn't matter how young or old your child is. This exercise works for all ages.

Sit on the floor across from your child. Look each other in the eyes for a few minutes. No giggling or talking. Just look into each other's eyes. Put your hands on each other's hearts, and as you do, tell each other that you love each other no matter what. Tell your child that you know without a doubt that they are perfect. Mean it. Take a moment to really see your child. Let your child see you without your defenses. Remember to breathe easily. When you feel like you are really connected, say a simple "I love you" to each other and see where it goes from there.

It's Time to Live Out Loud!

The Children of Now know truth, and they know when we aren't telling it. They can read us like an open book. Learning to tell the truth can be tough because we feel exposed, unsafe, when we do. The best way to go about recognizing your truth is to recognize *one truth at a time*. First of all, listen to your body. Find the deceptions inside of you. Change those untruths to real truths by getting honest with yourself. If someone is treating you badly, but you have made excuses for them time and again, why not admit that person doesn't show you respect? Even further, perhaps acknowledge that their treatment is abusive. Is that what you want?

If you have noticed certain behaviors in someone close to you, but you haven't asked that person about him- or herself because you don't *really want to know* the truth, or you have convinced yourself that you *can't possibly be right,* address this with yourself. Ask yourself what you are avoiding. What would the truth mean to you in this situation? What would the truth mean *really?* We tend to apply uncomfortable truths to ourselves in negative ways by feeling as if these truths were our fault somehow. Look beyond the reflexive reaction of somehow having been wrong and see the real dynamics. You may be surprised!

For instance, did you promise to go somewhere that you really didn't want to go to only because you wanted to be accepted, or maybe because you thought someone might not like you if you didn't go? *Don't go!* If you don't have respect for yourself and your needs, why would anyone else? You begin to get the picture. Honesty applies in every nook and cranny of our lives.

As you get the hang of inner truth, start practicing truth in the world around you. Put your newfound way of being into action. For instance, when you go out to lunch with your friends, and they suggest a restaurant where you really don't want to go, or if you are in the mood for something else, *speak up*. Suggest the place you want to go. Remember, you only get what you ask for! No one will hate you because you have a preference!

If you *really* want to eat elsewhere, and no one else does, be prepared to go to your selected eatery by yourself. Do it with love for yourself, not in a snit, and enjoy your lunch. If everyone in the family wants to go to the movies, and the one that they want to see doesn't appeal to you, but the one you have wanted to see for months is playing, go to the one you want and have a great time. Why sit through a movie you don't want to see? It's not like you are going to have a lot of quality conversation with everyone during the movie anyway. Again, go to your own movie with a smile, assuring everyone that it really is OK and you will see them after your respective movies.

With each small truth you tell, the greatness of your power as a human being returns. And seeing your example, your children learn to become true to themselves as well.

Real power is gentle power. It is not aggressive or threatening. It is all about living truth.

If you are truthful with yourself and others, and you are filled with integrity, then you become the power, and that power teaches you to fly.

The key to telling the truth is simple. But the message is entirely dependent upon its delivery.

In other words, how we say things makes a difference in how they are heard. If we feel threatened and send our words out in a jab, we are going to get jabbed back. If we deliver our message sincerely and without drama or trauma, that message will be heard much more clearly and as it was intended.

With each truth we tell, we take back our sense of self. Our children get our honesty and authenticity, and they, in turn, will take these qualities into the world, in all of their experiences.

Exercise: Where Is My Attention?

Find a place that is quiet and comfortable. Close your eyes and be still. Direct your attention inward. What do you hear? Is it the chatter of a million thoughts running through your mind, or something deeper? The chatter is part of your defense system that keeps the truth from reaching you. You created it. Now, tell it to be silent. If the chatter continues, ask yourself, where is my attention? Put your attention on you and nothing else. Listen to your breath. Inhale slowly; exhale slowly. As you breathe in, issue a command saying that you only want to hear the truth. As you exhale, expel the lies that have hidden within you. No more excuses, no more misinformation that leads you nowhere. Now, what do you hear?

You can do this exercise every day if you want. It only takes a few minutes. Remember to breathe as you direct truth into your life, into your very being. As you exhale, expel the untruths that you have held about anyone—any untruths that are keeping you from being who you are and who you want to be.

Exercise with Your Child

One of the things that keeps us from honest communication is fear of retribution or of being rejected or judged. Our children learn quickly to be silent in order to preserve their illusions of fitting in or not. This exercise is about setting a safe space for communication—a place where there is no threat of anything except that someone might listen!

This exercise can be done as often as necessary or desired. This author recommends making regular safe-zone appointments with your children and even other family members. Keeping communications open is 90 percent of a successful relationship of any kind. So here is how it works.

Get yourself and your child into a comfortable space or place—one in which there are as few distractions as possible. You will need to adjust this exercise a bit to allow for the age and maturity of your young one.

Tell your child that this space is your safe zone, that this is where each of you can talk freely, and no one will get into trouble or be punished for their feelings. The whole point is to learn how everyone feels, what they think, what they want to know. The possibilities are unlimited.

There are rules, though.

Rule 1: Everything that is said has to be said from a first-person perspective and not phrased as an accusation toward anyone else. In other words, "I feel that ...," *not* "You are ..." See the difference?

Rule 2: *Tell only the truth.* Everything that is said has to be honest.

Rule 3: *No arguing,* even if you don't agree.

Rule 4: If you aren't the one talking, *you have to listen without talking,* even if you don't like or agree with what is being said.

Rule 5: *No judgment.* If you are going to listen well, you can't judge what someone else is saying. What they are saying is their point of view, their feelings.

Rule 6: *No drama!* Yelling, screaming, crying, and playing attention-getting games are not allowed in the safe zone.

Rule 7: Everyone must *speak from the heart.* Being hateful doesn't solve anything, and frankly, when that kind of behavior starts, everyone else stops listening. Just speak with an honest intention of being heard and understood, or listen with the intention of really getting what others mean.

The goal of setting up the safe zone is to establish clear, honest, and safe communication between you and your child. A save zone can also work in relationships with adults. Our dysfunctional communication skills usually stem from immature responses from our inner child, who wants or needs to be right and feels as if they must be defended. In this setting, the inner child will not rule.

Either person present can begin by saying "I feel . . . (state the feeling)." For instance, you might say that you feel that you would like to know your child better—how they think, what their opinions are, what they feel that they need or lack. If there is something bothering your child or they have a beef with you, let them tell you without defending yourself. Just listen. When your child is finished talking, ask how you can help resolve the problem, if there is one. Listen to what they answer.

This is a time and place where communication is open and done with a tone of mutuality and honor. If you have any kind of a concern about your child, this is a great place to say it. Remember though, you can't express your concern from an accusatory or judgmental perspective. Just state the facts.

Once safe communication has been established, it will ultimately trickle into everyday communications. If an issue comes up that needs to be addressed, anyone can request a safe-zone meeting. When someone does, please honor the request immediately.

Good, heartfelt communication is the root of any successful relationship. Instead of teaching our kids to stuff their feelings, let's learn with them to get to the truth without feeling threatened or unsafe.

For little kids, sit on the bed or the floor with them and be fully present with them. Ask them how they feel about whatever subject occurs to you. Tell them your feelings too.

Keep in mind that children don't need a mature-adult or defensive, way-too-full explanation of anything. Just say the simple, honest truth in a way that is appropriate for their maturity level.

2

UNDERSTAND YOUR PURPOSE

It's not what you think!

Without realizing it, we often force our children to achieve, just the way our predecessors forced us. We overschedule our kids in the name of accomplishment, and we teach them to be like us. The problem is that we are so caught up in our own need to achieve that we don't even realize that we are running ourselves and our relationships into the ground.

We don't understand our purpose in life, so we continually fill our time with activities that make us feel successful or that we think give us value. Then why do we feel so empty? What are we missing? If we don't know, how will our children? We are creating neurotic kids by pushing them in fragmented directions. If we don't have purpose, then neither do our children.

The truth is that our purpose isn't singular. Value isn't really gained or measurable by our accomplishments in life. Instead, the success of our life is measurable by how we have lived it. Are we living intentionally, or are we flinging ourselves about, trying this and that? Are we appreciating the now, or are our minds and concerns all out in front of us, worrying about the future? Are we stuck in our past, regretting things, grieving, wallowing in what was? All of these things and more we teach our children by example. Teaching our children to live intentionally isn't hard at all once we have learned how.

So you don't know where you are going in life? You want so much, but in spite of your fantasies, nothing quite shakes out the way that you want it. You have felt for some time that you should be doing something different in your life. You have searched and searched, but don't understand what your purpose might be. You have asked a lot of people what they think you should do, but what they tell you just doesn't fit. That is because what they are giving you isn't yours.

To understand our purpose we must first realize one of the most significant statements that this book can offer:

Nothing ever happens outside of now. What was, has been. What hasn't yet been is merely imagined or speculated.

Let me repeat that:

Nothing ever happens outside of now.

This one little sentence can change your life entirely. Most of us spend all of our time worrying about what we did or didn't do or what might happen or not. Our attention is not now, but in the past or future. Creation is always talking to us. It communicates with us in real time, giving us state-of-the-art information as of this now, congruent and never ceasing. When our attention is elsewhere, we miss opportunities and signs that would have easily taken us to what we want. At the same time, when we aren't completely present in the now, the synchronicities, those magic little miracles in every moment, go unnoticed by us. We aren't grounded and are probably not even completely in our bodies.

How could we possibly know what our life purpose is when we can't even occupy a singular moment?

Life is nothing more than a series of singular moments tied together by events that create a sense of constancy that is filled with opportunity and experience.

All complexity is nothing more than an entanglement of simple situations.

The bottom line is that nothing is complex, and everything is simple.

Each moment is a simple situation. It only becomes complex or challenging when our perceptions make it so. Our children understand this concept innately, due to their innocence. As we lost our innocence, our minds were conditioned to defend us. Our minds actually are at work to defend us before our thoughts arrive and are recognized by us.

Communication is going on constantly. In and out, we receive and transmit information to all Creation, telling it what our experiences are and what we want. As we do, we literally expend and receive energy.

Because of these energy exchanges, we are literally never the same from one moment to the next. The symphony of our makeup has a few new notes or has changed rhythm. The same thing happens when we interact with other people. We exchange energy with them as we talk, as we express our emotions, and even our movements express energy and communicate. Others receive our energy, just as we receive theirs. As this exchange occurs, even with total strangers, we may never know just how much we have affected another person.

Our life purpose is not a singular event, but the collection of all that we experience in every moment that we exist. Each of us, in essence, is holding a particular place in universal reality. Because of this, each of us is a part of the balance of all that is. There is no other but you who can maintain your particular place within Creation.

*Each time that you interact with another, and each time
they interact with you, the exchange of energies changes
each of you forever. What you have given to them, and
what you have received, changes your and their energetic
structure in that moment. You may never know how you
have affected another in brief passing. Know this: you
may have changed their life completely!*

One of my favorite stories is that of a woman who was at the
post office to take care of some final business before going home
and committing suicide. As she stood in line, awaiting her turn, she
contemplated her death. Her husband, the love of her life, had died
unexpectedly, and she was devastated. Having been abandoned as
a child, and then adopted and abused mentally, emotionally, and
sexually by her adoptive parents, she had found salvation in her
husband.

He had been the first person in her entire life that she could
trust. He was the first person who had truly loved her unconditionally, and she him. Through him, she had learned about and experienced unconditional love, and now she had lost it. He was gone, so
today was it. She was definitely leaving the planet. No one wanted
her, she felt unrecognized, and . . .

Right about then a woman in the line next to her turned, met her
eyes, and smiled at her. The woman then turned around and went
about her business, getting her stamps and leaving. The distraught,
suicidal woman felt noticed. Someone cared enough to smile at her.
In the midst of her grief she had found an island of kindness, and
she decided that maybe life was worth living after all.

The previously suicidal woman ended up changing the entire
direction of her life and ultimately moved to a foreign country,
where she now teaches crafts to the locals so that they can supple-
ment their meager incomes. She also teaches English and jewelry-
making skills to children at the local school, and she assists the
villagers in their farming techniques.

That wonderful, kind stranger in line had no idea that her small gesture of kindness saved a very fragile life, or that her smile would lead to countless other lives being enriched.

All the result of one singular now. Wow.

We never really know how we affect others, especially our children. When we aren't present with them, they feel our emotional absence to their very cores. When we remember to act with intention, to mean what we say and say what we mean, we become that which we intend. *We also become the moment.*

As we do, every expression that we take, every thought that we have, every move that we make, each feeling we have, and every word that we say becomes reality.

Our purpose in life is not singular by any means. It is every moment that we exist. Our purpose is to live our lives freely, with grace and ease, embracing every moment joyfully and without fear.

Exercise: Learning to Be Now

Sit somewhere comfortable. Imagine that before you is a pyramid. The pyramid is a hologram and is created of light. Its sides look like liquid light, and they are a vibrant golden color. You can see though them, and the center of the pyramid is hollow. Project your attention to the inside of the pyramid. Breathe easily—in, out, in, out. You might find that your breath begins to cool. If it does, you have found the center of the pyramid.

Do you hear anything? A tone, perhaps? That tone is how you sound in all of Creation. It is your harmonic signature. Being inside of the pyramid allows you to safely experience yourself away from your body as a clear consciousness without the chatter of your mind. This space, this state, is you in clarity, unpolluted by earthly defenses. Stay here as long as you wish. Relax. Let yourself experience you without boundaries. You are safe. When you have allowed yourself to become the pyramid, you will have truly become the infinite now.

Freeing yourself of your defenses allows you to have more clarity in every moment, so that you are able to recognize the subtle signs that assist you to make more informed choices and to participate intentionally and honestly in every moment.

Exercise with Your Child

Enter the safe zone you learned to create in chapter I. Sit with your child. Each of you must be silent at first. Practice the art of observation. How does each of you look to each other? How do you feel to each other? Talk with your child about what you see in them. Ask your child to talk to you about what they see in you. These observations can be just surface things, like your pants and shirt don't match (or do), to deeper, more intuitive awareness ("You feel like you are sad inside . . .").

If your little one is a toddler or still very young, you can do things that are as simple as asking them to find their feet, their hands, objects in the room—anything that is in the present and available for observation.

If your child is old enough, you can do the pyramid exercise together. Modify it so that the two of you enter the same pyramid and experience each other as pure beings, touching your consciousness together. Connecting in this way, experiencing each other purely and without the everyday defenses present can be a profound experience between your child and you.

The point is to learn to be fully present with each other. How often do we cohabitate with others, but never really connect? Connect with your children!

3

STOP BEING AFRAID

You are sabotaging your life!

Fear underlies everything that we do. It runs our show from behind, driving us to make choices we regret, to miss opportunities, often to the point of grief for what was or could have been.

Some of the common fears we experience are:

- I won't be loved. *(Who would want to love me?)*

- I might be abandoned. *(No one loves me. No one wants me.)*

- I might be rejected. *(I knew I wouldn't fit in.)*

- My child might not get good grades or behaves badly. *(Will I look like a bad parent?)*

- I'll be judged. *(I am doing the best I can, aren't I?)*

- If I am not loved, then I will be alone. *(I am terrified of being alone!)*

- I won't succeed. I'm probably not good enough. *(Doesn't success mean being responsible?)*

- I don't deserve what I want. *(I am not worthy of what I want.)*

- I am afraid to bear responsibility. *(I don't know enough. I am not enough. What if I make a mistake?)*

- Someone might notice me. *(If I am seen, I am no longer invisible! Who do I have to be then? What if I screw up? I like being invisible. It is safer!)*

- I might not be a good parent. *(I have no idea what I am doing or how to talk to my child!)*

Of course, these are just a few samples. The list is endless. The truth is that:

Fear is not a reality—it is a what if. Fear causes the paralysis of our natural progression and is the cause of all failure.

We become afraid because we don't know what else to do. Becoming afraid is a gradual process that stacks one fear upon another, and each fear is gained through an experience we didn't like or that hurt us somehow.

Most of our fear is subconscious. Even though we don't realize it, fear drives our responses, behavior, choices, and even our life direction. We make our decisions with our fears biting us in the rear end, reminding us of our disappointments and our failures. Because of that, we often make choices that are not from a place of empowerment. Instead, we make our choices reflexively and without much thought. Our choices are based upon our history, patterns of behavior, and the underlying fears that result from our past experiences. These choices often lead us down a road that absolutely validates why we were afraid.

In other words, fear begets fear. It becomes a cyclic set of behaviors that become literal addictions. We make the same fearful choices over and over again, completely missing the fact that we are in a pattern of discomfort.

And then we wonder why things aren't the way we meant or wanted them to be. Further, we transfer our sense of fear to our children. They, too, learn to be afraid.

As we decide our life direction, do we take the easy road we are most familiar with, or do we take the high road, the one with more challenges and greater opportunities for the life we really want?

A lot of us choose comfortable discomfort.

We make choices from within our comfort zone, which really isn't comfortable at all. But it is all we know, and what we know is safe, right? *Wrong!*

When we choose from within our comfort zones, we are basically choosing from our past experiences, good, bad, or indifferent. We often choose from within our fears—fears that something bad might happen. Perhaps we're afraid we don't know enough to make a decision that might impact our lives greatly. Or if we *were* to make that decision and our lives *were* impacted, that would mean *change.* And *change is hard enough* without bringing it on directly, right?

Baloney. Take a chance. Take lots of chances. Choosing from within our comfort zone keeps life predictable and boring. Stretch. A lot.

If we are afraid, then we have the perception that for some reason we aren't safe at all! But the situations that cause our discomfort are predictable, and because of that we create a false sense of safety. It is generally the fear of the unknown that keeps us frozen in place.

Our false sense of safety gives us the illusion that we are in control of everything. We know what will happen, and what a relief it is to have life so predictable, so contained—*not!*

We sabotage ourselves on a regular basis by expecting certain outcomes to everything we do. When we have those expectations, we are living by a sense that we are in control of the outcomes. In fact, we are truly in charge of no one and nothing but our own choices and actions.

Control is one big, fat illusion. When things don't turn out like we expected, our fears are validated. Further, no one else knows what we expected, because it is our private little secret. Others don't have a clue how to participate with us. So in the process of trying to control everything, we instead create total failure because of what we had expected.

Setting ourselves up for failure of any kind, whether it is disappointment or reinforcement of our belief that we aren't good enough or deserving of what we expected, is self-sabotage. When things don't work out, our fears are confirmed, and we have proven to ourselves that all of our fears are true. By doing this we validate our fears, and they become larger, more ingrained in our subconscious.

Indirectly and directly we teach our fears to our children by the cautions that we give them or by not allowing them to do things or experience things because we don't want to see them hurt. Teaching our children to fear what we do is a disservice to their developmental process. Children need to develop based upon their personal experiences, not the ones that we put on them or give them. They need to learn healthy ways to process negative experiences so that those happenings don't haunt them forever. In order to allow our children this freedom, we must first learn to identify and conquer our own fears.

Your fear leaves you with a sense of powerlessness because you believe that others have more of something than you do. That is far from the truth. Still, you don't speak up when you disagree or want something different, because speaking up is too hard and you fear the consequences.

Further, staying in the victim role only serves to attract other bullies who will treat you exactly as you have invited. To believe that you are anything less than perfect is detrimental to your experience as a human being. You are perfection—hands down, no question.

Exercise: Identifying Your Fears

A word of warning: this exercise takes honesty. You don't have to be right or wrong. It isn't a test. At the same time, it requires a hard, honest look at painful experiences that you have had. This isn't about reliving the pain or even wallowing in it. This exercise is merely to assist you in recognizing the parts you play when fear presides over your life, and to show you how to truly become free of your fear.

To do this exercise, give yourself some privacy and approach it from a curious perspective. What has caused you to stay in your patterns? What have you been fighting all these years? What are your core fears?

Take a blank piece of paper. Begin to think of experiences that make your guts jump when you consider them. You know the feeling, that lurch in your chest. You don't like to think about these experiences because they hurt.

Usually when we have experiences that are uncomfortable, we blame those experiences on someone else or on something we felt we couldn't help at the time. This exercise is only about you—your feelings, your reactions, your needs—not what anyone else might have said or done.

Think of experiences that you have had that bring up that lurching feeling. Write the first one down that comes to mind. Not who did what or said what, just the experience. For instance, "This happened with so and so." Now look at it. Ask yourself why you participated in the experience if it was so hard. What were you fighting? What was your fear? What were you afraid might happen if you hadn't acted the way that you did in that circumstance? For all of those questions, you will derive one or two words that succinctly describe the fears.

Here is an example: "I was in a relationship that didn't work out. He left me with no explanation and went on to another relationship. I found out that the new relationship had started while he was still with me."

You might identify your core fears as:

abandonment
betrayal

Another example might be: "Everyone ganged up on me over something that I said, and I tried so hard to fix it. I was shunned and ultimately pushed out of the group."

In the margin for this experience you might put something like:

> *judgment* or
> *abandonment* or
> *fear of not being accepted*

The goal is naming the fear that drove you to do or feel something other than what you would have had you not been afraid. For instance, what fear caused you to allow the people in the above group example to push you away while you still wanted to be accepted by them? There was nothing wrong with what you said to them; others in the group just used it as an opportunity to gain false power. But there you were, fighting tooth and nail for them to accept you. And here you are, years later, still hurting over it while they have gone on with their lives and probably don't even remember the event.

Go to the next event in your life that brings up that awful physical feeling. Repeat the process until you have addressed all of the situations that you can think of.

When you are finished, look over the fears you wrote down. You will find that the same words repeat over and over again. These are your core fears. Now that you have recognized them, owned them, you can let them go. Have compassion for yourself for allowing these fears to run your life, and make a pact with yourself that you are done with these fears.

The next time the patterns try to come up, you will recognize them immediately and choose from your power rather than your fear. Oh, and have a sense of humor about it. Laugh at yourself when you find those fears creeping up! You now know better! You aren't hiding from yourself anymore! The best news is that once you are aware of your fears, no one else can hurt you there anymore. This is living from within your vulnerabilities. If you have owned your fears, no one can use them against you.

Learning to be unafraid frees us to experience our lives to their fullest potentials. Further, when we are not afraid, we can communicate with our children honestly and fully. A lack of fear allows for open communication without editing!

Exercise with Your Child

Our children are not born with innate fears. Fears are learned. The fears kids express are often about something that they have encountered or believe in, like monsters under the bed. To a child, speaking a fear makes it all too real, so they tend to suppress or hide their fear. No matter what the age of your child, toddler or teen, get in your safe zone and talk about fears. Again, be careful not to get too deep into adult conversation when expressing your fears. But candid discussion goes a long way in bringing things out in the open and allowing them to process out.

Teens can use this exercise along with the previous one for adults. Careful guidance will help your child realize that their fears are usually over something that has blown up out of proportion inside of them, because they have thought about it over and over, but not spoken of their fear or let it out. Encourage them to talk about these fears, even if the fears seem silly to you, and then suggest, without judgment, how the fear is unfounded. If the fear is legit, then take whatever action is necessary to relieve your child's stress.

4

RECOGNIZE YOUR PATTERNS

Those things we keep doing make us
who we are, and we never notice!

Patterns are behaviors or situations that repeat throughout our life experiences. They are behaviors we have developed or been taught, and they are our typical response to external situations, as well as to our internal feelings. Patterns are our built-in self-defense mechanisms that keep us within our comfort zone. Call patterns our knee-jerk reactions, if you will. Patterns are what happen when fear rules our roost.

Situation Patterns

Patterns are situations that come up for us over and over again to challenge us to make a different choice, to act in a different way, or to either commit or run like heck. They are opportunities for us to change our ways completely or in part. Each time a situation repeats for us, we are being asked to choose again. Will we again opt for what we know, or will we try something different? The choice is ours. Patterns also denote underlying fears we have not dealt with. The patterns cycle through our lives, giving us opportunities to make a different choice, to change our response to a given situation, or even to conquer our fears.

Somewhere inside of us, we are aware of these repetitions in our experiences, and even when we aren't OK with them, we let them continue because we don't know any other way or that we have a choice. The problem with having life patterns is that because we have them, we often develop certain types of personalities that lead us to different types of dysfunction.

We must learn to recognize our patterns. There is a good chance that patterns come from within our family's example of behaviors. We commonly replicate the behaviors we learned as children, and we usually pass those very same patterns on to our kids. Often, we learn by example, and those examples aren't always particularly healthy for us. Yet we duly model those examples to our children subconsciously or because on some level we think that our patterns are normal and therefore must be the right thing to do, right? Not necessarily!

Patterns are situations that repeat time and time again. They may have different faces on different days, but they are all bear the same theme and the same dynamics.

For instance, our relationships with others often bring out very recognizable patterns. How many of your friendships have left you saying something like, "Why do I always attract these kinds of people? The same kinds of situations happen over and over, and I just don't get it! Why is everybody like that?"

You attract these friendships because over and over again you are choosing people who give you the opportunity to choose differently! As soon as you make a different choice, the patterns stop. As long as you react the same way over and over again, those same types of opportunities will come to you over and over again until you get it. It is really that simple.

Repetitive issues are another good example of patterns that we often encounter. Issues of honesty or integrity or betrayal are the most common. How many times have you been in a situation where you felt that someone took advantage of you? Maybe they borrowed money they never paid back. Or maybe they weren't true to their word. Maybe you felt betrayed by what they did or didn't do.

Just when you think things are going well, it happens again on another day and with another person. *What aren't you getting?* In this case, fear, which has created a lack of self-worth, has conquered you once again.

When we don't value ourselves, we are sitting ducks for others to mirror that very lack of worth back to us!

They treat us as if we don't matter; they treat us as if we are less than or don't know as much. We get taken advantage of—again.

The mirroring that we receive from others is exactly what we feared in the first place. Worse, we become victims of our own creation!

If you don't value yourself, why should anyone else? The patterns that you have created with your fear will spiral over and over again until you have conquered your fear— or succumbed to it.

Patterns are quite predictable when you step back and really look at your relationships and your habits. Once you have recognized your tendencies and have awareness of your fears, then no one can hurt you there anymore. It is what you won't look at or can't see that gets you into trouble time and again.

The beauty of recognizing our patterns and becoming re-sensitized to the possibilities at hand is that we can share with our children what we are learning as we learn it. As our kids witness our willingness and openness to change, they will inevitably be willing and open too.

Defensive Personality Patterns

When we experience patterns, such as repetitive experiences or repeating relationship issues, we will often develop personality patterns as well. These personality patterns take many forms, and we are generally oblivious to them.

Our defensive personality traits can ultimately limit our life experiences in a major way, or even keep us crippled emotionally and in maturity. These defensive traits are often passed down to our children. Our children become just like us as they mature because they think our behaviors are normal. But we want our kids to be themselves, not to act from who we are or who we think we are. We want them to be everything that they can be.

Here are just a few types of personality patterns that you may recognize in yourself or someone around you. Of course, there are more, but these are the most prominent behavioral patterns that are often born of fear.

The Victim

Victimization is a pattern that can be broken only when the victim has had enough abuse and is ready to become something other than a target for others wanting to feel more powerful.

Abuse is any behavior that is disrespectful to you, dishonors you, or is meant to make you feel as though you are not as good as or are less powerful than someone else. If you are displaying the Victim role to your children, you are telling them that it is OK to allow others to treat them that way, and they will ultimately allow others to do so.

If you are a Victim, either in a relationship or life in general, break the pattern. Stop doing what everyone else wants. Start telling your truth even though doing so may be one of the scariest things you have ever done. Stop deferring to others or another. Speak up! Act out! Honestly, if your abuser doesn't want you or love you once you have become your authentic self, they never really did want or love you, at least not in a healthy way. You deserve more than settling for what you have, and the greatest gift you can give yourself is the acknowledgment of self. Begin to reward yourself for even the smallest of successes. Recognize and embrace that part of you who really does want change. Give yourself some credit.

The best way to change your life is to change your mind!

Fear causes us to develop belief systems that are disempowering. When we begin to believe something different, not only does our entire perspective change, but our lives also change!

Sometimes when we are acting a Victim role, everything seems impossible. It seems difficult to stand up and make the change. This is, of course, not the truth. The truth is that anything is possible if we believe it.

Sometimes though, powerlessness sneaks up on us. We become embroiled in it slowly until one day we look up and can't see our way out. We are in way over our head with mixed feelings and emotions. We want to think the best of people, but they aren't acting rationally. If you are one of those people who feel that your situation is out of control to a dangerous point, such as in a physically abusive relationship, and you feel unsafe and that your situation is hurting you, please get help. Not your best friend's help—help from people who will keep you safe in the transition. Many different social-service agencies offer counseling, safe houses, and any number of possibilities for a person who wants to gain control of his or her life. Whatever you do, get out of your situation and know that there is no excuse, period, for anyone, ever, to treat you that way!

You deserve only the best of everything. You are a child of Creation, made of the same stuff that all others are made. Therefore, there cannot be anyone who is lesser or greater than *you!*

You have the inalienable right to experience life on your own terms. That is your birthright. You didn't come to this world to be insignificant. You came to experience life at its fullest!

Being a Victim has no rewards and a whole lot of pain.

Being a Victim means that your fear is paralyzing you!
Stretch your being toward the powerful soul that you are!

The Do-Gooder

Another pattern of behavior that keeps the truth out of the way is what I call the Do-Gooder. The Do-Gooder spends most of their energy doing for others in a selfless sacrifice of time and personal resources. The Do-Gooder can't sit still. Doing for others is a way of avoiding personal pain and issues. Do-Gooders work mostly on the surface, smiling the whole way and appearing selfless, but they are really hiding their inner feelings by keeping the focus on someone else's problems. The Do-Gooder waits on everyone hand and foot, helping them clean up their personal messes, and is generally working hard to be the good girl or boy. And everybody loves them. We all like free stuff, and the Do-Gooder has a bucketful!

Being a Do-Gooder brings a false sense of value or accomplishment. The Do-Gooder goes home at night all puffed up, feeling valuable for all they have contributed to others. In the meantime they haven't done anything much about their personal stuff. By doing for everyone else, by living the reality that others are creating, Do-Gooder brings to heart a false sense of reward.

We create situations so that we can learn from them. Sometimes those situations are very hard. When we get ourselves into these messes, we know exactly whom to call: the Do-Gooder! And bless their hearts, Do-Gooders don't remember how to say no, so they will drop everything in their own life to rescue the troubled friend or family member—or total stranger.

What the Do-Gooder doesn't realize is that by carrying the weight of a situation that someone else has created, they are literally robbing that person of the fullness of the experience that person created in order to learn and change.

Later on, the person who was in trouble and got bailed out by the Do-Gooder will inevitably call again with similar issues or troubles because they didn't learn the first time and because someone rescued them!

You see this pattern a lot in families, as well-meaning parents rescue their offspring over and over and then don't understand why that son or daughter continues to get into trouble. This pattern is a great source of heartbreak, and it is brought on by denial.

For instance, a grown son can't seem to hold a job and regularly goes to Mom and Dad for an infusion of money. Mom and Dad feel sorry for their son who "tries so hard," and they give him the cash, with a lecture about getting a job. And the cycle repeats over and over again. The son doesn't learn and neither do the parents, because to them, giving him the cash is the right thing to do! They have enabled their son not to work, and they've picked up the pieces of his mess. He hasn't learned a thing except that someone will bail him out later when it happens again!

Becoming a conscious observer removes you from the drama and the trauma and allows you to see things for what they are. Instead of running to the rescue all of the time, the greatest way to assist is not by doing for someone, but by giving them the tools to help themselves. For instance, you can make suggestions toward resolution: "Here is where you can get what you need," "Here are some ideas about how to make this situation different," or "Here are some observations I made the last three times that I helped you with similar problems." And let them choose to resolve their situation or not. Make them responsible.

Doing for others doesn't give you value—it enslaves you.

The Do-Gooder is really only placating that good little girl or boy inner child who never really felt enough recognition. The key to breaking the Do-Gooder pattern is giving yourself fair recognition and giving up the need to get the kudos from someone else. Give yourself the value that you give others, and you won't need to get it from anyone else. Pretty soon saying no won't be so hard!

The Taker

Opposite to the Do-Gooder is the Taker. The Taker is one who has, for whatever reason, become a dependent personality. The Taker is needy and does not believe that they have what it takes to take care of themselves on all levels.

Takers generally are very personable and love to talk. They sit back and, consciously or subconsciously, watch for opportunities to get what they need from others, instead of getting it by themselves. They will become your best friend, and it will cost you.

People become Takers because of a fear of real commitment. They fear commitment out of a deep sense of self-loathing, which keeps them from thinking they are good enough to commit. At the same time, self-deception has instilled a false sense of self-worth somewhere along the line.

Takers are not at all honest with themselves. They are users and completely convinced that getting something from someone without giving back is the absolutely most right thing they have ever done. Takers not only take emotionally while wearing a mask of authenticity, they also use material things to give them value.

Takers manipulate to receive material things from others as perceived "rewards" for being such a nice person, or being present in general. They feel quite deserving even when they are not. They will have a thousand excuses why taking is right—if the situation is ever discussed. But deep down inside, Takers are afraid to commit to doing whatever it takes to be a success. They feed off of the success of others. Taking becomes a pattern.

What Takers get is false fulfillment, not realizing the things and emotional rewards do not make them who they are. Things and stuff are used to replace true depth of emotion and experience and Takers are left feeling unfulfilled, lacking, and in need.

When a Taker runs out of potential resources with one person or group of people, they will develop a new set of people to draw from, abruptly leaving the original group wondering what happened and where the Taker went. If asked, the Taker will mumble some lame excuse and bring up a different subject with the usual charm. Moving around a lot so as not to be discovered is part of the Taker pattern.

Takers aren't lazy; they just truly don't have the self-worth or self-confidence to dive in like everyone else. A Taker is envious because they have not yet realized that the power to create is within. To give to a Taker is to enable and perpetuate the habit of taking and, worse, propagating their illusion of false value.

If this pattern sounds like it fits you, the best thing that you can do is to begin to empower yourself by following through on even small commitments when you have no agenda of receiving something in return. Begin to become empowered by first admitting this is your pattern and then learning to give. Give to yourself from the inside out by learning to acknowledge your real value. Learn not to expect anything from others. Up until now, you have held on to things and stuff because you see your value in them. Things have no value if you don't value yourself. Look past the voices and the old tapes that play in your mind that tell you that you are only valuable and acceptable if . . . and to the truth of you without all those learned perceptions. You are only what you believe—as long as what you believe is the truth.

The Loner

Another difficult pattern to break is one I call the Loner. This pattern is based upon the fear of being hurt (again!). It is also fear of having one's emotions exposed, the fear of being discovered. Often Loners have developed the perception that showing one's feelings is unsafe and leaves one vulnerable.

Loners dive into books or isolate themselves, holding in feelings to the point that they show little outward expression. The amazing thing is that when these people speak, the depth of their awareness, observations, or knowledge is often a great surprise to others. There is much lurking deep in there!

The Loner fears showing feelings or expressing thoughts that someone else can then judge or use against them. The Loner thinks the safest thing to do is to be quiet and unavailable—invisible. Of course, this kind of behavior may accomplish the need not to be discovered by self or others, or the need to avoid engaging to any depth with others, but it really limits life experience. After all, when Loners protect themselves and limit their experiences because of that protection, they don't let in any stimulus that might feel unsafe or painful. At the same time, this same behavior also limits the depth of how life is being lived. In other words, what the Loner is protecting on the inside by not letting in what feels unsafe, they are also missing in the way of life experience. They don't accept that the fullness of experience involves others, and the Loner pattern is propagated. Life becomes a series of fantasies or dreams that, even if participated in, are never quite enough.

The Loner fills their time with distractions, such as a good book, or analytic behavior. Everything needs to be understood so there are no surprises. But there always are.

If you are one of these delicate people, start putting yourself into small situations that stretch your comfort zone.

Let yourself be seen, even if you are not comfortable.
What you will find is that when you are, you are beautiful.
People will like you because they are able to know you,
and your hideout won't beckon so loudly.

The Bully (aka the Know-It-All)

Another behavioral pattern that arises from fear is, believe it or not, the Bully, also known as the Know-It-All. This behavior comes from deep fear of not being good enough. These people usually comes from a family background in which they were seriously disempowered by a parent or parents who were of similar personality. The general tendency is to cover all sense of vulnerability by becoming omnipotent, bigger than life. This tendency often manifests as rudeness, loudness, and acting as if their way is the only way, no matter what cost it is to others.

The Bully or Know-It-All will sometimes act as if they truly do know it all. This affectation covers up the fact that they are absolutely terrified of being wrong. Criticism infuriates them, because they often don't recognize or admit their deep insecurities. Even though they don't really know everything, they have convinced themselves that they do, and they talk right over anyone who tries to express an opinion.

The Bully will bark at others from the perspective of absolute righteousness that is related to their opinion of how things are or should be done. They have such a sense of self-righteousness that they often cause hard feelings in families and social circles. And then a secondary pattern, the Victim, manifests, as the Bully wonders why no one wants to be around them or why everyone is mad at them.

When facing this kind of personality, people tend to avoid in-depth interaction so as to avoid a confrontation or an argument. In other words, they let the Bully or Know-It-All be right because acquiescing is easier than dealing with the consequences of acting otherwise.

On the other hand, the Bully or Know-It-All is also, at times, a very generous person. With a fanfare, they will surprise you with presents or money. They are gregarious people who are hard to avoid. On the inside they have a lot of pent-up emotion, feelings that have not been expressed because, again, expressing them feels unsafe. The Bully or Know-It-All is generally a marshmallow inside when you get past the façade.

If you recognize yourself in this description, my suggestion is that you learn to relax. You no longer have anything to prove. Your pain is not serving you and is generally sabotaging your relationships with others. No one is watching over your shoulder anymore. The only person that you must please is yourself. Be gentle with yourself.

You are a powerful and magnificent being of Creation, and that is good enough. Learning to be truthful with yourself is the number-one priority. The second priority is to learn to have compassion for yourself. If you can find compassion for yourself, you will have it for others and will begin to understand that damage that is done when you bark at them or overrun them with your perceived power. Learn to laugh at yourself. It is never too late.

The above examples are just some types of personality patterns and their behaviors. The kinds of patterns we develop are endless, but, for the most part, are familiar to all of us. If we can develop an awareness of those patterns, we can also begin to recognize our fears. Fear isn't reality. This now is. When we stop being afraid, we stop propagating our fears. And we don't share them with our children. When our children are unafraid, they have the potential to dive into life and to achieve far more than they ever would have by living familial patterns.

Exercise: Defining and Changing Patterns

What kinds of situations repeat for you and have over the years? Do you attract the same personality types and then find the relationships unbearable? Are you experiencing similar behaviors from your friends, loves, others? Have you ever said something like "I guess I have to keep doing this until I get it right"? The answer is likely *yes!*

Once you identify your situations that are repetitive, ask yourself how you can react or respond differently next time, because there will be a next time. Once you change how you react or respond, the pattern will stop.

Exercise with Your Child

Your child will begin repetitive-behavior patterns early. These patterns may involve not doing homework and thus setting themselves up for failure, or self-sabotaging themselves by getting into trouble or losing important items such as school assignments and thus proving to themselves that their poor self-image was correct.

If you notice that your child is repeating certain behaviors that lead to discomfort of any kind, first help your child recognize the pattern. Then help your child realize why they are behaving that way in the first place. For example, the reason could be something is happening at school, and because your child doesn't know how to deal with it, their discomfort is coming out in other places and behaviors. Kids are generally easy to read if you are paying attention! The key to this exercise is parents' or caregivers' awareness of the children on a day-to-day basis.

5

REMEMBER YOUR PASSION

I'm stuck, I'm bored, and I really want to find it!

If we don't know what we love, then how can we teach our children to be passionate about anything in life?

Much of our sense of misdirection in life comes from the sense that we haven't got a singular passion. But why do we need only one? We think that passion has to be in one direction or kind of experience, that one thing will make us happy, successful, and filled with joy, if it weren't so elusive. Passion is intangible, and therefore difficult for us to imagine.

Sometimes we think of passion much in the way that we think of the voice of God: as a booming, unmistakable, all-encompassing blast from the heavens. We think of passion as total bliss that fills us to the point of making us fall to our knees.

Just in the way that God doesn't shout at us in his huge voice, passion is often more subtle. Passion is often a feeling that starts in our very core, slowly (or quickly, depending upon the circumstances) fills our heart space, and then overflows outward through our bodies.

Passion is what we love. It is the feeling that fills us with joy and releases our emotions with such magnitude that we have to express them or we will bust. Remember how on Christmas morning you were filled with excitement as you ran to see what Santa had brought? Or how, when you got your first bike, you felt so big? Or how you felt when you had your first kiss? Passion is like that. Passion comes from innocence. It is so pure, so light in nature that it is easily buried by external influences and even by our inner experiences (how we deal with things, if we do at all). Passion can also be depth of Spirit. As we allow ourselves to be in a place of feeling all that is sacred, we are overwhelmed with grace, a feeling that both humbles and empowers us and often brings us to a point that we can barely stand. (I think this power of grace is why we may have originally had to kneel in church. When this kind of passion is felt, there is nothing else to do but crumple under the beauty of it and to become immersed in Spirit.)

Passion can also be pure love—for another person or group of people, for an activity, or for the sheer beauty of our world. Passion for another person can be profound when it is pure and allowed to come to the surface. What we feel when we look into the eyes of our children is a form of passion; we want everything for them and would do anything to protect them. Becoming so engrossed in an activity that all time seems to stop and our mind clears and we are fully present in the now is passion. In that presence we are experiencing actual living of our passion. Experiencing the intricacies of nature, each aspect of our world being created in a way that it is both separate and dependent, is a form of passion. Look at the human body, for instance. It is a complete biosystem that has multiple parts, each with a purpose and all dependent upon the other.

We can experience passion through the senses of our body as we can see and feel beauty, we can hear the intricacies of a symphony, we can taste fully every culinary experience, and we can smell the fragrance of a rose, the air after a fresh rain, newly cut grass or what scents come riding on the wind. Each experience that we have with our bodies is a moment of passion. Those moments are tiny vacations from the tediousness of life. They are moments of complete presence, clarity of experience, and fully loving what is happening to us. When we choose to stop and experience these little moments, we are living passion.

We have the ability to choose what we do or experience, the ability to move about in our world and to experience as much of it as we desire. We choose how we feel and what we want, all the while our bodies continue to support us, as long as we give them the care that they need.

Religions create passionate belief.

Essentially, passion has many forms all around us. And we experience it only when we release the bondage that we have created and allow ourselves to feel and express completely the fullness of our hearts.

A lot of us seem to feel that we are not living our passions, that we are in a mundane life that seems to be status quo each day, predictable and lacking in depth. We want to feel inspired. We want to feel as if we matter, and we want to live fully. Yet there we sit, day after day, accepting life as the cards have been dealt. *This is a travesty!*

If we are to experience our passion, we must first give up the preconceptions that it is something to be obtained. Passion is within us 24/7. It is ours, and it is infinite.

To be passionate is to stop guarding ourselves and to come out of emotional hiding. Hiding who we are is betrayal of self.

Most of us believe that passion is our purpose and that we have to achieve that purpose, whatever it is. Our passion is not our purpose—it is our *right*. It is who we are when we let go of the illusion that we are separate and different from everyone else and allow our sacred selves to surface.

There is a vast difference between direction and purpose. Many people have gotten to the point that they are no longer excited about most things and often feel complacent, even morose, about their current circumstances. They have become so enmeshed in the herd, in being like everyone else, that they are lost to the point that they don't recognize their greatest motivational aspect, their passion. Now what?

We have learned that our purpose can be found in every moment, each now. But what about our passion? Our passion leads our direction, guides us, motivates us, and brings us pleasure in everything that we do.

The first question that I ask people when they are feeling lost in life is, what is your passion? The truth is that about nine and a half out of ten people don't know how to answer.

Passion dictates our direction when we allow ourselves the freedom of feeling to great depths. Passion allows us to give ourselves over completely to what we are doing and to our emotions. It fuels us when we are tired and releases chemicals in our bodies that make us feel terrific. Passion gives us spring in our step and the ability to spring out of bed in the morning with anticipation of a terrific day.

So why is it missing? How do we find that big elusive feeling that brings exuberance to our everyday experiences? To do so, we must first understand why our passion is so hard to come by.

How We Become Desensitized

We live in an information world. We get global happenings in practically real time, all of the time. As we witness wars and disasters, crime and punishment, indifference, overpopulation, undernourishment, disease, weather anomalies, and more, part of our psyche turns away and closes down. We have too much coming at us to maintain the kind of sensitivity that we had in previous times.

At the same time we are emotionally closing down to the horrors in our world, there are ads and commercials blaring at us. Try watching a program on TV these days. There are more commercials running across the bottom of the screen distracting us than there are original programs. Information is plastered on buildings, billboards, bus and taxi signs, taxis, and, in fact, pretty much every available surface. These ads tell us that if we buy a certain product, it will make us beautiful, worthwhile, comfortable, loved, smarter—all of that and more. There is so much to see that we begin to doubt ourselves or simply tune out the visual overload. At the same time, our psyche believes some of those messages because color and movement, flashes of small bits of information, all register on subliminal levels and convince us that what the ads are saying is true. Those ads literally contribute to the alteration of our belief systems.

With the Internet touting pretty much anything we want to read, see, or hear, and with chain stores, banks, restaurants, and others filling every available commercial space in nearly every country on our planet, we are becoming desensitized to our own unique cultures. In fact, we are being deculturalized, losing our traditions, our rites and rituals, as we try to fit in and in many ways try out other cultures and their practices as spiritual changes. These efforts contribute to our desensitization because as we cast about we lose the depth of spirit and emotion that our own cultural traditions bring us. Almost everywhere we go, there is something familiar in our face. The cultures of our world are becoming blurred and blended, and our traditions are going by the wayside as their sacredness somehow gets lost in the bigger picture. With travel as easy as it is these days, people go all over the world. There is very little "us" and "them" anymore; instead there is a collective us, all of whom are after basically the same thing. This is not the same as being one with all things; this general "us-ness" is about denial. Denial of lineage, of tradition, of culture, of spiritual beliefs, and even denial of feelings. We've lost exuberance in exchange for the mundane. By contrast, when we operate as intentional aspects of the one, we create excitement, mutuality, and at the same time catalyze personal expansion. The world is much more interesting.

The world population is out of control; some people are starving and going without basic needs, while others waste everything, but because we are safe in our backyards, have plenty to eat and more available, we don't even notice the pain and suffering of others. We are numb to it. Schools are beyond overcrowded, and we have all become numbers instead of human beings with names and lives and families. For our children, every day becomes a survival challenge of body, mind, and spirit. Our kids learn to filter out all "extraneous" people and begin feeling isolated in the process. They become insensitive to the emotions and pain of other children and especially to the adults around them. This kind of self-protection leads to isolation and disconnection or disassociation.

There are drug ads everywhere, implying that we need something more than what we have and that we need it to be chemically induced. They tell us that we should talk to our doctors to obtain the drugs. They show healthy, happy people swinging without a care in the world, and make it seem that taking drugs is the best thing for our life experience. These drugs only serve to contribute to our desensitization.

The corporate world in general employs scads of people in a race that no one can win, completely forgetting that it is the human element that keeps its wheels going. We've become so focused on performance that we tend to forget about human interaction. This kind of environment of fierce competition leads to situations of betrayal, deceit, and more.

In order to survive such a dog-eat-dog work culture, it can seem necessary to desensitize toward coworkers and to focus only on our own results. Or, conversely, some people desensitize by focusing on what everyone else is doing in the office and not on themselves. Either way, people are losing touch and become too stressed, too sick, too tired to have any quality of life.

Our children become further desensitized by video games, movies, and other activities that take them into fantasy worlds and out of their own exquisite lives.

With our sensitivity bashed and battered, we become emotionally shielded. We forget to nurture ourselves, and we become closed. How can we feel passion when we are numbed on a daily basis by the entire world coming at us?

Relighting Our Fire

First of all, we have to stop being so emotionally guarded. We hide our emotional expressions because we feel vulnerable, exposed if we show our true feelings. We try so hard to hide how we feel that we practically explode at times.

It is time to bring our vulnerable selves into the world, lock, stock, and barrel. When we operate from within our vulnerabilities, no one can hurt us there anymore. We reign, unchallenged, within ourselves. When we have identified our fears, as we have learned to do in chapter 3, owned those fears, and embraced them, we are no longer vulnerable except to our own perceptions.

Coming to the world honestly and without the old baggage brings a forgotten lightness to our experience. Honesty allows us to begin to feel again many of the emotions we had buried, stuffed, and forgotten. Letting go of fear frees us to feel infinitely and further to act on our feelings from the perspective of an innocent child.

We must recall what brought passion to us in our past, in our childhood, when we were innocent and not guarding ourselves defensively from life. A fun way to begin is to think about what you loved as a child. What brought you joy? What made you smile? What games did you play, stories did you tell, jokes did you share? OK, so maybe you had a difficult childhood. What were your fantasies when you were a kid? What were your dreams and aspirations? Did you role-play? Act out your favorite superhero or TV star? Who was it, and what was it that you admired about them? You stopped doing those things only because someone decided that grown-ups can't play. Tap into those feelings. Let yourself grin.

Most of the people whom I have assisted with this subject have immediately identified passion as having to do with other people. This saddens me. From my point of view,

passion is an internal experience that brings animation and fulfillment to the expression of outward experience—life!

Passion is a lap full of puppies, the birth of a child, great love with another or even our self. It is a classic movie that jerks the emotions all over the board, leaving us with a face full of tears. Passion is our spiritual self, that self that is limitless in heart and depth. Passion is a great conversation in which your ideas are challenged and from which comes the inevitable "aha!" moments. Passion is love and anger, grief and compassion. Passion is the penultimate emotion, second only to love. Passion is anything and everything that you love.

Quite frankly, if you aren't feeling it, you are doing for everyone else and haven't realized that receiving is just as important as giving. When we give and give without replenishing our resources, we get tired to the core. When we are emotionally unfulfilled and tired, we cannot find the depth of feeling that we know exists. To change this, we must learn how to command what we need and then to gracefully receive it.

Receiving is about value. If we don't perceive ourselves as valuable, we receive very little in comparison to what we might have gained by valuing ourselves. We get only what we believe we deserve. In other words, if we envision ourselves as lacking, then we become lack. Lack finds us. After all, everything that we seek seeks us. What we intend is truth—or at least it is our truth. So learning to receive isn't that hard. It is about giving yourself an hour or two (even if you have to make an appointment with yourself) and doing something that brings you joy. If that is as simple as a walk in the woods, fantastic. Having a massage—being safely touched and relaxing completely, with the focus on you for a change—is wonderfully nurturing. Sitting by a creek, with the water flowing and the sun reflecting off the water, can be extremely cleansing and nurturing. Feed the ducks or the fish while you are there. Let yourself merge with nature or into the dark or in the sun. It doesn't matter what you do. Just feel. That feeling is a spark of the very passion you seek.

Find reasons to laugh. Laugh for no reason at all. If you are laughing, believe it or not you are almost there.

Passion is laughter that has become systemic.

Passion is alive. It is living emotion that courses all through your body, mind, and soul. Passion is like that. Passion fills every molecule of every cell in your body with definite direction or an etheric pause, if that is what is needed.

Do you *have* to have something to be passionate about? Honestly, no. Passion is a state of being, not something to do. If you let your guard down and stop defending yourself, let the tension ooze out of your body, you will find that capacity to feel much more deeply than you knew you could.

If you feel that your passion needs direction, what is it that you have always wanted to do, but have not ever done? Do *that*. Do something exotic, like a hot air balloon ride or a midnight sail.

Passion applies to work, too.

If you do what you love, you will love what you do!

When we become passionate, this passion overflows into everything that we do. It becomes a positive expression of the intensity of love that is within us. When we find our passion, it is contagious. Our children recognize this passion and respond in kind instead of hiding their feelings. They learn to express themselves without defense, fully and completely and from their hearts. Their innocence remains intact even as they go out into the world. They laugh instead of internalizing their everyday experiences.

Exercise: Find Your Heart and Open It

Physically or mentally take yourself to your favorite place. What is it that you love about that place? Is it there that you are able to relax and let go of stress? Are there things there that you love to do, even if that means doing nothing? Let yourself sink into that place.

Next, close your eyes. Go back in time. Think of instances when your heart was full. When your child was born, or before that, how you felt with your first love—anything that brought that feeling of swelling into your heart and soul.

Bring that feeling forward into this now. And as you do, breathe deeply and intentionally, allowing your heart space to swell fully. As you exhale, let go of the tension that had guarded your heart.

Maintain the feeling that you have found buried in your being. Breathe again, locking that feeling in place.

When you find yourself raising your guard, losing your focus on self, bring your attention back to your heart and breathe that feeling back into place. Carry this feeling into everything that you do.

Once you have found your heart, stop several times throughout each day and breathe that feeling through your body. Pretty soon you and your heart feeling will become one and the same!

Exercise with Your Child

Playing is a fantastic source of self-expression. Children play naturally. Think of something that you liked to do as a kid or that your child loves to do now, but that you really haven't participated in. Do that. Do it from the perspective that you are the same age as your child. No, I don't mean talk like that or get into that posture. Just let the little kid inside of you. Play with your progeny as an equal.

You will very likely feel silly at first, but keep going. When you play, you let down your guard and become more authentic. Being authentic is a great way to get in touch with yourself and develop a fuller relationship with your child!

A water hose is terrific fun. Make sure you get squirted as much as your children! Race across the yard. Fly a kite together. Play tag. Whatever you would like. Encourage your child to express their glee, and let them be as expressive as they want. And encourage yourself to do so too!

6

QUESTION EVERYTHING!

You don't know as much as you think you do!

Kids question everything! Especially around age three or four, they want to know "why" about everything. They are trying to find reasons for the complexities of our world. As adults, we forget to question or simply don't bother. We just muddle along, knowing that the rules must be for a good reason or situations are as they are, and we don't challenge anything the way we could.

It takes a lot of energy and attention to pursue lines of questioning and, frankly, a lot of people would rather do something else.

Let the child within you ask questions about anything and everything. You aren't in charge of your experience as long as you go along with the herd!

When our children ask us those who, what, where, when, and how questions, they are unequivocally stating that they are interested in what is going on and they want to learn more. Because we may not know all of the answers to our children's questions, or maybe we haven't even answered those very same questions for ourselves, we often tell them to stop asking. We teach them to be quiet and stop being so curious. In doing so, we teach our children to fit in the box of normal and not reach for the golden ring of life.

Our kids don't ask questions for no reason. Generally, some thought, experience, or series of thoughts led them to the moment of query. How can we take advantage of that moment and teach our child something valuable? How can we teach them to find answers on their own?

Having questions is about learning, not about having answers and not about judging. It doesn't matter if we know or not what our child wants to know. What really matters is what we do with that moment. Judging ourselves as adequate or not doesn't get us anywhere. And remember that everything we are challenged to teach our child is something that we need to learn or remember ourselves!

Instead of giving our kids pat answers or telling them to stop asking so many questions, why not show them how or where to find their answers? How about answering them by asking more questions and letting them deduce their own answers and opinions?

We become uncomfortable with their questioning because we feel that they are being intrusive at times. That is because we were taught to mind our own business and that children should be seen and not heard. Another reason that we are uncomfortable with questioning is that many of us would rather remain invisible, to not be noticed or challenged. Plus, answering all of those questions takes a lot of energy that we don't always feel we have!

Learning to feed our own curiosity leads us to be more open to new and different ideas, as well as to the experiences of others.

One thing that gets us into trouble time and again is ignoring the obvious. We don't ask enough questions. Asking questions doesn't mean getting trapped in an analytical pattern that makes you lost and even more unaware. What it does mean is to become intentionally aware.

Becoming the Conscious Observer

In chapter 4, I mentioned becoming a conscious observer. If we are to live intentionally and to be what we intend, don't you think that we have a responsibility to know what we are really experiencing, what people are really saying, and what the real dynamics are in our interactions with others?

Being a conscious observer does not mean setting aside your emotions and looking at the world from the perspective of a drone. What it means is to observe from a step back, to notice what is going on without getting ensnared in other people's issues or in the drama of a given situation.

Often people are not saying what they really mean, but we believe them because they said so. Later we find out that they didn't mean a word of it and they were only making words to please us (or themselves) in the moment. Their actions speak volumes, and what those actions say is different from their words.

If we had been consciously observing in the first place, we would have seen that perhaps they didn't meet our eyes directly, or as they made a promise their bodies turned away from us. These signs would have clearly told us that they weren't telling the truth or didn't really mean what they said. But we heard what we wanted to hear, and now we are in a situation that is not OK.

How about the times we ourselves have reacted with anger, flouting our temper and being defensive when it wasn't necessary? We saw or heard something and made too quick an assumption, only to be very sorry later.

Being a conscious observer means stepping out of our reflexive, guarded behaviors and into a place of calm observation.

This takes practice. Our tendency is to have knee-jerk reactions based upon our past experiences. But let's be honest; if we are still reacting to the past, we aren't where we want to be. We aren't reacting from who we are now and that can get confusing! It is time to change our interactions to those of power and truth.

When we allow ourselves to observe without prejudice, we begin to experience the truth, no matter what.

Time and again it is our predisposed assumptions and our neediness that get us what we don't want. If we can watch with a new set of eyes and really see what is happening, we will find out that not everyone is as honest as we would like to think. Not everyone means what they say.

Conversely, there are a lot of people we never gave a chance because there was something about them we didn't like. Chances are that whatever we didn't like about them was very similar to something we didn't like about ourselves or feel unsafe exploring! As we observe with our new eyes, we also become more present. Remember, being in the now is a huge leap to our new life. We begin to see new and exciting opportunities and avoid the pitfalls of going down a deceptive road. How we see everything is a vital part of our new way of being. When we learn to observe consciously, the possibilities hidden within every situation can easily blossom into reality, because we paid enough attention to act on them as they were revealed.

Learning to Be Discerning

Discernment. What a concept! You mean, we have the right to decide what is good for us? You bet! Not only the right, but also the responsibility. When we discern for ourselves, we are really choosing whether or not a situation, information, an idea, or even a social norm fits us and our needs.

There are a lot of people in our world who will sell us a bill of goods in a heartbeat. There is a lot of misinformation out there. The question is, what applies to us and how do we know?

Discernment may seem difficult at first because the old habit of lying to ourselves may creep in. So often we find ourselves wanting to believe what we are seeing or hearing because the way we are seeing it is the way we want things to be. We want someone to give us the answers to life. We want someone to tell us how to make things easier. And so we listen to them because we think we hear them telling us what we want to hear. We lie to ourselves, brushing off obvious falsehoods because we want to fit in so badly that we're willing to cling to what they tell us even when it isn't even close to what we really feel. We see someone who is clean, well dressed, and purported to be an authority on a particular subject, and we take their words as gospel. We spend our days trying to be who they told us we are, only to find out that their ideas about how we should live our lives are far from our inner truth. Those ideas may have worked for that person, but they certainly don't work for us.

On the flip side, we are suspicious of everything and everyone because we don't know how to trust others. We are afraid to trust. So we discount our experiences as a bunch of hooey and go about what we do know, often missing golden opportunities because we reacted a little too quickly.

If we learn to be discerning, to observe consciously and intentionally without jumping to action or conclusions, we begin to experience the honesty we wish to create.

There are a few great questions that you can ask yourself to give yourself a reality check. The first one is:

How do I really feel about this?

Taking the time to listen to your body can save you a lot of grief later. Is something nagging at you that you just can't put your finger on? *Trust that feeling! And act accordingly!*

Am I in truth?

Check your honesty. Ask yourself if you are telling yourself the truth or just what you want to hear. Becoming aware of what is really going on inside of you is vital to an acceptable outcome.

Is this mine?

This question alone can save you years of grief. Often we take on the feelings or problems of others because that is how we allow ourselves to be set up in a given situation, especially situations that sizzle with differences or high emotions. Often we take responsibility for the things that others do or say just because we were there. The thing is, everyone is always making choices and reacting from their own sets of perceptions. Everyone has motivations and issues, and they make choices based on them. Just because someone chooses to react in a certain way, even if that reaction is negative, their behavior isn't ours to carry. On the contrary, when we are a conscious observer, we can see that behavior for what it is, smile, and go on our way. So make sure that the situation or feeling that you are about to address is actually yours. After a little practice, you will find that you were reactive to many situations that were someone else's all along!

We tend to want to fix things so that we don't have conflict in our experiences. Uncomfortable situations are scary, so we do all that we can to avoid them. Or we take on guilt, anger, or other negative emotions that really don't match how we started out feeling. If you find yourself becoming agitated in any situation, ask if what you are feeling is yours. Then be truthful. Sometimes someone is mirroring to you, and your buttons are being pushed. If that is the case, own your discomfort. Treat it as an opportunity to recognize something inside of you that's been hidden away. Then, set that new truth aside until you can look at the issue clearly and uninfluenced by others. If what you see in reflection from another person is not yours, don't try to own it. Acknowledge the other person's behavior, know that it isn't yours, and get on with life.

Is action required?

Is what you are consciously observing pulling you to act in some way? Do you want to jump into something because you are excited? Or do you want to run because the situation is making you uncomfortable?

Have a look at your inclinations. Should you really jump? Do you know enough to make sure the pool is full of water, so that when you jump in, you don't hit concrete? Do you really have enough information to act?

Are you uncomfortable because you haven't been honest with yourself or because the situation really isn't good for you? Once you have honestly considered things, then choose to act or not.

What is my responsibility in this now?

Often we feel it is our responsibility to act on behalf of others or we are led subconsciously to react out of guilt or discomfort in a certain way.

You are now officially off the hook. Responsibility is a choice, not an obligation.

Whatever you choose to do, do it because it is really what you want to do, not what you *should* do. If you find yourself thinking you *should* do something—anything—have a serious look at why you are doing it at all.

As our children begin to go to school and move through the socialization process, they can become confused between following the rules, fitting in, and other people's issues. It can be pretty overwhelming suddenly to be around a lot more children and adults than they are accustomed to, and often a lot of unfamiliar behaviors. They face rules that don't make sense and are often created simply to control the masses. At the same time, the values they know so well from home are often challenged, and they don't understand why they have to act in ways that seem unnatural to them. It can be very confusing for a child.

For instance, when I was a child in grammar school, we were expected to sit at attention. That meant sitting straight as an arrow, with our hands folded on the center of the desktop, feet planted squarely in front of us, and it was darned uncomfortable. When the teacher called us to attention, it meant that no one dared talk or continue with anything that might distract them from what the teacher was about to do.

Children are sensitive to the dynamics of motivation and behavior of other people as well as whether or not others possess good coping skills. Children know what others really mean, and they become confused when the truth of what they know is contradicted by the outward behavior of others. Being a conscious observer will help our kids find the freedom to experience their life processes without being enabled by others who encourage them to accept less than their inner truth. When our kids learn the difference between their internal stuff and the stuff of others, they can keep from forming inappropriate attachments to other people's behaviors, and thus save themselves a lifetime of disappointment and pain. Further, our children can more clearly focus on what is important to them, and they will be more at ease in every kind of environment.

Exercise: Five Questions

Think of three recent situations in which things turned out not to be what you thought. Look at one situation at a time, and discern how you could have acted differently or chosen to react in a way that had a greater benefit for you. As you look at each situation, ask yourself the five questions in this chapter. Answer yourself honestly. You will find that your perception changes greatly based upon the questions. For your convenience, here are the questions again:

> *How do I really feel?*
> *Am I in truth?*
> *Is this mine?*

Is action required?

What is my responsibility in this now?

Exercise with Your Child

Part One: As situations come up, use the above five questions with your child. For instance, your young one comes home from school and tells you a story about an event that happened that day on the playground. A bully has beaten up your son's best friend, and your son feels responsible because he couldn't do anything to stop it. In fact, he was afraid he would be next.

"So how do you really feel?"

What do you mean?

"Do you really feel that your friend getting hurt was your fault?"

Well ... no ... but ...

"So is it true that it was your fault, or are you just feeling guilty about something that you couldn't control?"

Well, yeah, I guess that is more like it ...

"Does that mean then that this is your problem to carry around?"

What do you mean?

"What I mean is two big boys beat up your friend. Just because you were there doesn't mean it was your fault. Feeling like you can't help it is a normal feeling in a situation like that. It doesn't mean you did anything wrong."

Well, I didn't. I was just standing there talking, and they came up behind Jason and knocked him down and then threw dirt in his face.

"Is there anything that you should do about this?"

What do you mean?

"Is there any action that you should take so that this doesn't happen again?"

Well, I don't want to be a tattletale ...

"Oh, so you would rather just avoid these guys all year so they don't make you their next victim?"

No. I would rather be friends with them. I would rather have them on my side than against me and my friends.

"Well, that is a creative approach. First of all, when you make friends, it is because you genuinely want to be in their company. Make sure that when you make friends that it is for all the right reasons—not because you need or want something from them. Friends are special people who we choose to have in our lives. They are a lot like family. Jason is your friend. Do you feel that you have any responsibility because you didn't know how to help him?"

Well, looking at it like we are, no, I don't. I didn't make anyone act so mean, and I sure didn't push Jason down. I helped him up and took him into the restroom, so he could get cleaned up. I was just being his friend.

"Yes, you sure were! So after looking at this more closely, do you still feel the same as when we started talking about it?"

No, I really don't. I see now that none of this was my fault. I did the best that I could, and so I don't feel as sad as I did. But I do feel sad that Jason got hurt and that some people act mean ...

"Maybe showing those boys a different example, like how you helped Jason, will teach them about kindness. You know sometimes people are mean just because they are really scared inside and they don't know how else to be."

This is a healthy way of processing a situation that could have stayed with your child indefinitely.

Part Two: Play questions tag with your child. One of you will ask a question, and then the other has to answer it (truthfully, of course). As long as your question is answered, you get to go again. As soon as your question isn't answered by your partner, your partner gets to ask questions. The questions should be meaningful, not just to be silly, as should your answers. There is no winner or loser, just a good awareness that questioning everything is OK and that listening to the answers is just as important.

7

BE AUTHENTIC

Who have you been kidding anyway?

Children's needs are best met by parents who have met their own needs. Often we live superficially, trying to be who and what we think everyone wants us to be. We are living life from a dysfunctional perspective, one where we are uncertain who we are and what we mean to be in our lives. We send our kids very mixed messages. We aren't consistent within ourselves, or if we are, we are consistently repeating old patterns and tapes that run in our subconscious, forcing us to behave in ways that are unpredictable or, at best, predictably unbalanced. Now, I am not talking about neurosis. I am talking about the inability to live life from an honest perspective from the inside.

When we live this way, we show our children the very things that make us uncomfortable in our lives. We show them indecision, knee-jerk reflexive behaviors, unstable emotion, and even tendencies to participate in unhealthy relationships that validate our very belief that we are far less than perfect. Our children begin to pick up those behaviors, at least unconsciously. As they get older, our children become us in many ways. We absolutely need to be who and what we mean in our lives.

As an approach to improving our lives, we fervently work toward "healing" ourselves, toward becoming some idealistic version of a human being. We read self-help books, follow a certain behavioral protocol that is supposed to optimize our experiences, take workshops, go to lectures, buy gadgets and products that are purported to change our lives. But do we really know who we are or what we are trying to accomplish with all that grueling effort?

Do we have to suffer our past miseries to be who we want to be? Do we have to participate with others in their drama and trauma to get to the place we mean to go? Are we who other people say we are? *No, no, and no!*

How can we shake loose all of the things that are really holding us down? How do we find those issues in the first place? This chapter is about realizing a definite direction and how to be what we mean, with ease.

Even though we are intrinsically perfect and magnificent beings of Creation, what we believe has everything to do with who we are. If we see ourselves as less than perfect, we must be so. If we see ourselves in need of something, we must be. If we see ourselves as unsatisfied, we feel unfulfilled. If we believe that we lack, then we do.

Look in the mirror. Who do you see? Your mom? Your dad? A grandparent perhaps? Look further. Meet your eyes in the mirror. Beyond the physical, who is looking back at you? *You are.*

A soul embodied and incarnated for an experience of L.I.F.E.:

Living

In

Fullness and

Excellence

But we believe differently, so we don't see, feel, or experience our excellence. Changing our lives is as easy as changing our minds. Perspective is everything.

Perceptions are an imaging system that human beings utilize to define experience. In order to change the experience, one has only to change the perception.

The Clock Exercise ~ Here is how it looks!

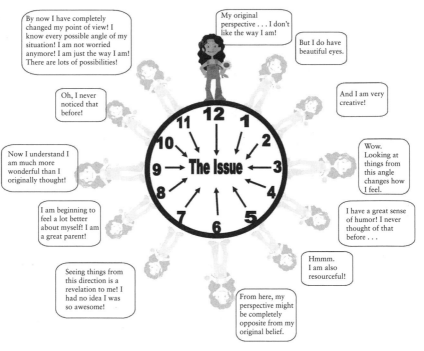

FIGURE 1. THE CLOCK EXERCISE

In order to be who we want to be, we must change our belief systems. An easy way to do this is to picture the face of a clock with all of the numbers present (see figure 1). Picture yourself in the middle of the clock, where the hands are connected. The twelve o'clock mark represents your current perspective of yourself in the center of the clock dial—everything you believe about yourself in this now.

Absorb what you believe about yourself. Once you have a good understanding of your present view, imagine stepping over to the one o'clock position. From this perspective, your point of view changes. See yourself from a different angle. If you believed that your body was imperfect, see now how beautiful your fingers or your eyes are. Absorb this new perspective.

Then imagine moving over to the two o'clock position. See yourself again through new eyes. If you thought that you were perhaps not a success, begin to look at the moments in your life that you were one.

Continue around the face of the clock. With each station, find a different way to see yourself. Some of the things that you see may not be what you would consider positive. Take note of those things and have a look at them from another perspective or number on the clock. How can you change your point of view so that you see yourself differently?

This wonderful exercise can be used for any subject. You can even make a clock on the driveway with chalk, or in the yard or living room with whatever you have handy. Always start at twelve o'clock to begin your explorative journey.

When faced with tough or even everyday decisions, it is always a great idea to use this process or one like it to weigh out consequences before jumping into action. To learn to see all sides of yourself and your life as well as the issues that come up takes away the feelings of panic or inadequacy that often occur. You are no longer acting reflexively but instead from a balanced, secure perspective.

Other People's Stuff

Often when we look in the mirror, what we see is what others have told us or implied.

*Just because someone expressed an opinion or made a requirement of us **does not** mean they are right or what they say or believe is true. What they see isn't us, but a reflection of all that they believe.*

What you know is truth. What you remember is the extension of that truth beyond measurable limits. No one else's truth lives your life for you. Only yours does.

Modeling ourselves after others is a terrible disservice to the real us who is clawing to come out! But we do model ourselves. Over and over again, we say, "How do I look?" "Did I do a good job?" "What should I do about . . . ?" "What do you think about . . . ?" "Did you hear about . . . ? It could have been us." And on we go, begging for validation, feeling the need to have someone else approve of who we are and what we do.

Let's be honest here.

Everyone who tells us anything does so from a perspective that they have developed over the course of their lifetime. That perspective may or may not be functional or even healthy.

Yet we want so badly to see ourselves looking terrific in other people's eyes. Generally, what people mirror to us is what we *don't* want to see. For instance, we see a trait in someone that we loathe. It bothers us so much that we go off-the-wall mad at them, even if they are perfect strangers. If we were really being honest, we would see that maybe we have a little bit or a great deal of the same trait, but we just didn't want to admit it. It is easier to project our beliefs outward to others and blame them. The problem is that *they are only as aware of themselves as they choose to be.*

So here we are, looking at others to be our mirror, to reinforce our confidence, to know who we are and what we are about, what we should do and even how to do it, not realizing that they don't have a clue who they are, what they are doing, or even how do gauge themselves any better than we do! Geez! *What are we thinking?*

OK, from now on you are off the hook. You don't have to care at all what anyone else thinks, says, or does. You only need to look inside, from whatever perspective you want, and you will decide what your experience is, what you will do, and who you are. When you can do that, you can begin to be free.

No More Worries

When we aren't afraid anymore and we don't need anyone else's opinion about anything, we begin to feel glimpses of freedom inside of us. We begin to act from a less convoluted perspective, one that is ours entirely and dependent upon no other influences.

Now, what is there to worry about, really?

Worrying is like leaning out in front of yourself, looking for trouble that doesn't exist.

Since you no longer need to care what anyone else thinks, says, or does, you no longer need anyone else's approval. If people do have judgments about you, they are coming from their stuff, not yours.

So when others try to bait you, to draw you into the illusion of imperfection, you don't have to go there. You don't have to believe them because you are none of what they accuse you of and everything that is perfect! Imagine teaching your kids to have the freedom to be who they are in any given situation. What kind of people will they be? It all depends upon the example you give them.

As you perfect this new point of view, amazing things begin to happen. You become authentic. You are no longer afraid. Your vulnerabilities are no longer your enemy. No one else's opinion matters. You no longer need to compare yourself to others. *You are becoming **you**!*

As you step into your authenticity, you convey the message to your child or children that it is OK to be who they are. They will learn that conforming to the whims and opinions of others isn't acceptable or desirable. They will gain an internal strength that will allow them to have the confidence it takes to be whomever and whatever they choose.

Exercise: Take a Walk with a Different Set of Ears

From your new set of perspectives, take a walk downtown, in the mall, at the ball field, or wherever there are a lot of people. Listen to your inner thoughts as you walk. *Where is your attention?* Observe yourself as you move through the crowd.

Can you catch yourself becoming judgmental? Comparing yourself to someone else, based on what they are wearing, how they are acting, what they are saying? Really pay attention. Be the conscious observer. Remember that if their opinions about you don't matter, neither do your opinions of them! What matters is the conscious observation of others and how you internalize or express what you witness. You can begin to feel like an island of peace amongst all of the external chaos.

Exercise with Your Child

Take the same walk with your child. Make an agreement that this walk is not about talking, but about listening and observing. Instead of forming opinions about anyone or anything that you see or hear, you and your child are to just listen and feel what is happening on your insides.

From time to time, compare notes. What did you observe? How does each of you feel? What did it feel like when you saw people have certain behaviors? What made you happy, sad, or uncomfortable? Talk about how each of you reacted to what you experienced, not about other people. By doing this exercise, your child can learn that they are responsible for their own experience.

8

HAVE A SENSE OF HUMOR

When did life get so serious? Laugh!

Oh God, do we ever need to laugh! But we don't do it enough. We spend so much time all tied up, not letting our true feelings out. Laughter literally releases body chemicals that are great for our health and well-being. so why are we frowning? Why are we so tight? Does life have to be so doggone serious all of the time?

We are still protecting our inner child, one who is historic, but still whining in the background. How do we comfort that child, and how do we break free from subconscious immaturity?

One of the attributes that we gain as we mature is a sense of responsibility to ourselves and others. We are given the instruction and impression that responsibility takes a certain appearance and that if we are not responsible, we are failures. As we become more and more responsible, we begin to lose our innocence.

Amber Alert! Help! I've Lost My Inner Child!

About the time we enter puberty, maybe even a little sooner than that, we begin to notice what everyone else thinks of us. Recognizing what others (particularly our peers) think of us becomes one of the most important aspects of our development. Their views of us become our focus, their approval our goal, and those opinions affect our general perception of our self. Our innocent sense of self begins to fade, and we want to be all grown up.

We begin to dress and act according to others. We begin to talk like our friends, using inflections, expressions, and phrases so that we fit in. We begin to wean ourselves from our families to a large degree, and at the same time, more and more demands are made of us. We are becoming older and therefore must assume more responsibilities. More expectations are made of us, and consequences generally follow if we don't meet those expectations.

Later we are required to find a job, some kind of work to contribute to our growing expenses and wants. Our jobs have further requirements, and our time begins to belong less and less to us.

Some of us continue our educations and move away from home to go to college. There, we must meet grade-point requirements, we are tested in a pass-or-fail manner. We are expected to choose a field of study—what we want to do for the rest of our lives—at a young age. We have to make lifelong commitments to things we aren't yet even familiar with, let alone passionate about.

In the process of all of these changes come relationships and ultimately a love with whom we may even create a family. That family needs to be supported, and we are the breadwinners.

We go to work, we come home, and everyone has needs and demands. We lose touch with our inner selves and often give up altogether on our passions. There just isn't enough time.

The lives we had so looked forward to become a conforming blur of everyone else's needs, wants, and desires, and there doesn't always seem to be room for extracurricular activities that we love or want to do. What a gruesome picture! The lives that we so anticipated and the milestones that we wanted to achieve ultimately become albatrosses around our necks.

Lighten Up!

We have to laugh. Being serious about everything is against our nature. When we don't laugh, it is because we are guarded. We have built defensive walls all around us. To some people, laughter is considered silliness or even a weakness. These perceptions come from the same perspective that prompted us to guard ourselves in the first place. To others, laughter means emotional exposure. If you find something funny or humorous, you might be showing too much of your private self.

The truth is that the more we laugh, the more we are willing to come out and play, the more balanced we become. This doesn't mean that we have to shirk our responsibilities. We just need to take a different perception about ourselves and our place in our world.

We have to lighten up!

It isn't as hard as you might think. How many times have we nearly busted a gut trying not to laugh because we thought laughing wasn't appropriate at the time? Laughter is a release mechanism that reduces stress and tension and allows us to be authentic. The truth is that when we don't laugh, when we hold it inside in the name of being appropriate, all of those feelings will come out in the form of hysteria at the wrong time.

I remember being a young adult and carrying my guardedness around like a trophy. I was determined to fit in and be everything that was expected of me. I thought I was impenetrable. Everyone thought I was so strong when on the inside I was a marshmallow. I was in great need of emotional support, but I had little to none. Being that protected all the time was hard work, and I wasn't particularly happy in general.

My brother was engaged to an extremely volatile woman, and I knew the match would never last. My son had been requested to be the ring bearer in his uncle's wedding. He was just a little guy, maybe three or four years old if that. He was so cute in his little tuxedo and was very proud to have such a responsibility.

The morning of the wedding, as the bride was getting ready, she was an absolute terror. She was screaming profanities and yelling at everyone in her presence. She had an idea of just how her wedding was going to be, and she was determined to have that vision at everyone else's expense. One particular point of tension for her was that her veil wasn't staying put. She had been to the hairdresser, and whatever had been put in her hair had made it so silky that the comb of the veil couldn't sit well. That her veil was precarious made her even more aggressive with everyone. Her behavior was so raw that it was painful to be around, and I ultimately left the room.

The bride finally seemed to have everything put together, and the wedding began. There they were, the bride, my brother, the attendants, and my little guy, who stood right next to the bride with his tiny pillow, proudly holding the soon-to-be-worn rings. Partway through the ceremony, my son wanted to say something to the bride.

So he began to tug on her veil. It was all he could reach.

All I could think of was how she was going to lose it if her veil came off. It was an extremely tense moment. And I started to laugh. God, I tried so hard to hold it in. And the more I tried to stifle myself, the more I laughed. I was hysterical, laughing so hard I was crying. In a vain effort to become invisible in my uncontrolled laughter, I literally laid down between church pews. And I still couldn't stop.

And he tugged on the veil harder. Oh God.

My laughter was contagious. Several people around me saw what was going on, and they started to laugh at me. What was I going to do? Ruin my brother's wedding? I was sitting in the very front of the church, so leaving while I was cracking up wasn't really an option.

Well, I just couldn't help it. I laughed until I cried. And the more I realized that I was out of control, the more I laughed. I was so embarrassed, but I just couldn't stop laughing. Somehow, in spite of me, the wedding took place, the rings made it onto their respective fingers, and no, the veil didn't come off. I don't know why.

Looking back, I realize now that that moment was a bit of hysteria and a trigger for me to let out years of frustration and trying to hide my true feelings. In what seemed like an interminable few minutes, my body had released more chemicals, had released more pressure than I had even been aware I had. What a relief!

Then I had to beat myself up for being so inappropriate. But after I got over myself, I was able to laugh about it. I still do. Somehow, contrary to all of my fears of dire consequences, no one ever said a word! My fear of repercussions was all in my imagination. It was as if my laughing bout had been invisible and inaudible. Everyone was so caught up in the wedding that I had gone entirely unnoticed except to myself and a few people around me who had great senses of humor!

Allowing ourselves to become bottled up emotionally only serves to create an emotional pressure cooker that, sooner or later, has to blow if we don't take the lid off. When we are self-defended and don't laugh, soon we feel that we are unfulfilled. We begin to feel spiritually and emotionally empty. We look to others to fill this place inside of us, or we try to fill it with stuff and things of a material nature. None of this helps, but we keep doing it. And we teach our kids to hold it all in. Is that what we want for them?

Letting our emotions flow isn't as hard as we think. To do so, we must simply return to our innocence. The child within us is anxiously waiting to come out. Inside, each of us wants to come out and be free.

Getting Beyond Serious

Beginning our journey back to inner freedom requires us only to get in touch with the child within us. For some of us, that child may seem to be flailing, unsupported, abandoned, unloved, or, worse, even abused. Even if that is true, the child within us *can learn* to feel safe and free. We are that child, and we do know what we want, what we need, but we have denied ourselves these things for what seems like forever.

So maybe as kids we really didn't have what we needed emotionally. Or at least we perceive that we didn't. That was then. Now we can choose our experiences. The question is, what do we need now, and why aren't we getting it? We can't look to someone else for our laughter or for our inner freedom. We must stop seeing ourselves as wounded or broken, and instead take on the new perception that we are perfect in every moment.

When we hold in our emotions, one of the first things that happens is that we stop breathing, literally. Our bodies become tense, and for a moment we are paralyzed in our existence until we take our next breath. A great way to move past these kinds of moments is first to become aware of them and second to take an intentional ten or twelve deep breaths several times a day to relieve our tension. Breathing also helps keep our energy, or chi, flowing more freely.

If, as we breathe, we can also imagine the child within us and all of its emotions, we can direct our breath to our inner child, nurturing it. As we breathe life back into our inner child, we can allow our hearts to expand and begin to love that child fully and unconditionally, the way it always wanted to be loved.

As we become more and more aware of the feelings of our inner child, we become more aware of just how guarded we became and even perhaps what it was we were defending. We find basic, raw emotions born in the heart of our inner child. Oh, how we needed! And who noticed? We did. Do we notice what our children need? Are our children aware of what they need?

Awareness is the key to relaxing in ourselves.

Awareness creates perceptions. What we perceive is based upon our awareness of the now in combination with our history. Our egos become involved, trying at once to bolster our opinions of self and at the same time destroying who we think we are. So let's move past our ego.

Our general reaction to the demands of life is to buck up and do our best to win approval. It happens at work a lot. The boss comes along and drops a bomb in our lap in the form of a project that needs to be completed within a ridiculous timeline. It is inconvenient and nearly an impossible task, but we are so grateful to have been noticed that, after an initial hesitation, about a split second, we gratefully accept the responsibility and immediately go about doing the best job ever—even though that means working day and night for perhaps weeks. On the due date, we confidently march into the boss's office with the completed project in hand. It is the best work we have ever done. Instead of getting the kudos that we secretly expect, we barely get a nod of recognition. We feel let down and empty. But then it isn't the first time. The child within us is devastated, and so we continue to try harder. The problem is that all of that trying is really at our expense. No one else really notices, or if they do, they are often jealous and accuse us of being the favorite or a brown noser. Geez!

In the same vein, our children work very hard to get our attention, our praise, and to know that they are loved completely. They compete with their siblings for more attention from us. Ultimately, there is an argument between the child and their siblings, which we are then expected to moderate, or we correct what seems to us to be inappropriate behavior, and our child's secret fear that we don't love him enough has been validated, even though he created the situation.

When we are kids, we develop patterns like this as we do our best to become noticed, validated, and, yes, even loved. These patterns carry into our adult lives much like the example above, yet somehow we never seem to get what we want or need. That is because we are looking to others to fulfill us.

In order to find our senses of humor again, we must become present with ourselves. As we do, we can become aware of the moments that our bodies tense up and we stop breathing. These physical reactions are huge clues that in this moment we are defending ourselves. From what? Why?

Well, the reasons really don't matter. What does is finding compassion for ourselves. And then laughing about how serious we think we are. And then laughing again and again, releasing a lifetime of tension in this beautiful way.

What is it that you dreamed of as a child? What were your favorite activities? What brought you a feeling of empowerment? What were your favorite activities? Games? TV shows? Movies?

Do those things again. Take yourself back to your fantasy worlds. Touch the freedom of those moments. Buy a kite. Blow some bubbles and watch them reach the sky. Imagine yourself riding one all the way to the heavens. Get a can of silly string and ambush someone. Make sure that you have a can ready for them as well. Stomp in a mud puddle with both feet. (I did that recently and shocked everyone present. Their eyes got big, and no one knew how to respond. It was fantastic!)

Whatever it takes, let your inner child be free.

Your inner child isn't subject to anyone's approval but yours. Most of all, instead of putting yourself down when you feel that you have screwed up, laugh, laugh, laugh. The mistake doesn't matter to anyone but you.

Exercise: Come Out to Play

Think back to how you played as a child. Do that. Invite some friends if you want. Get a game of Twister and a couple of pizzas and have a slumber party, pajamas and all. Buy a quart of bubbles and go outside and ride your imagination away with each tenuous orb. Buy a couple dozen cans of silly string and start a string war. Play jacks. Hide and seek. Do whatever you loved to do when you were small. Whatever you choose may feel silly at first. You will find that you are stiff in yourself. Relax. Have fun. How much fun you have is always up to you.

Practice laughing even if you are alone. Laugh out loud. From your belly. At anything and at everything. Release your inhibitions and begin to feel the rhythm of your true emotions.

Exercise with Your Child

Our children learn from us and the other people in their environments to take life too seriously. They begin to edit themselves based upon what they believe is expected from them. Soon they have learned to keep their feelings inside. Further, they are encouraged to "not talk back" or not to express their opinions. Because of this they lose their spontaneity.

This exercise is ongoing. When situations come up and your children are disappointed in themselves, encourage them to find the humor in the situation. Encourage them to learn to laugh at their mistakes and to learn from those mistakes rather than to become discouraged. Take time out of your day to play with your children. Laugh with them. Show them that there is a child inside of you who loves to come out to play.

9

SEE THAT CHANGE IS MAGNIFICENT

And stop being so resistant!

Change is an expression of our willingness to live to our fullest potential. It is the impetus for wider experience and greater depth of feeling. Change is necessary if we are to break out of our complacency and step boldly into our lives and all that they may bring.

Children are some of the most flexible creatures on this earth. At the drop of a hat, they will twist and turn in whatever direction life takes them. Emotionally, they tend to recover much more quickly than adults. Children are the first to see the good in everything. Now don't get me wrong. Children also need structure in their lives and can be forever damaged on emotional levels if not nurtured well and properly. They need to know they are safe and what to expect. My point is that our kids are very, very adaptable with life's changes as long as they know that change is OK and that often those changes lead to even greater life experience!

Our children's ability to change directly mirrors the examples they are given. When they see the adults in their lives resisting change, they learn to resist too. They begin to believe that change is a bad thing and that they should force their life situations toward their intended end no matter what. Forcing life situations toward an imagined outcome generally causes more problems and an undesirable outcome. It is this kind of behavior that creates control issues later in life.

If we are to give them a good example of how to be more flexible, we must first become more pliant ourselves. Sometimes we refuse to give in just for the sake of resistance because that is the way we have always done things.

What if, in that moment of struggle, we caught ourselves and really looked at why we are fighting against something different? Is the potential change really a bad thing? Or are we resisting it just because we have always done things the current way? Or is resisting change a reflexive, subconscious behavior that is the only way we know? How else could the way we do things be done? What would happen if we did do something different? Hmm. The possibilities begin to seem endless.

The first thing we do when faced with the opportunity for change is to kick and scream and resist like a coyote caught in a snare. We fight, we howl, but when the inevitable change comes anyway, there we are, suffocating in our resistance. The more we refuse to give in to change, the more stagnant our experience of life becomes.

Stagnancy leads to resignation, and resignation leads to surrender. Surrender to the idea that we have been dealt a lot in life and that is all we get. So there we sit.

If we put a voice to our resistance, it would sound something like this: "Oh, poor me. I am not willing to change a thing. I am afraid of what I don't understand. If I allow this change, then I am not in control anymore. I want it my way. Why, oh *why*, don't I get what I want *just the way I am?*"

Oh brother! Want a little cheese with that whine? As if we are ever in control anyway. It's hard to have sympathy for an attitude like that, yet how many of us really do have that mind-set? The truth is that just the way we are is magnificent. Once again, how we perceive ourselves has everything to do with the experience of who we are.

What we know, what is familiar, is our safety zone. It is, as we discussed earlier, often our comfortable discomfort. The only way to truly leave that zone is for change to occur, even if that change is only within us. Inner change is the greatest change of all.

Change is a choice. Sometimes, though, change carries us through no apparent initiative of our own. Sometimes when we have resisted long enough, seemingly uninvited change comes in like a north wind, clearing everything that is an obstacle to our growth and taking us expediently to entirely new circumstances that are unfamiliar and require us to alter our previous habits and thinking.

*Change forces choice, but change also **is** a choice. You have the power to change your existence right now. There is no change without chaos. There is no chaos without a catalyst. You **are** the catalyst. And the result of chaos is magnificence!*

When We Are Open to Change, Miracles Happen

What is a miracle anyway?

A miracle is an event or action that is amazing, extraordinary, or unexpected. A miracle may seem contrary to the laws of nature or to be an act of God.

Miracles are happening all around us in every moment of every day. They are the little surprises we get that are expected, but are perfect in that now. When we are feeling down, and someone right then tells us how amazingly perfect we are. When we are out of money and wondering how to make ends meet, and we get a check in the mail that we didn't even know was coming. When our children say their first word or take their first step. When we say the absolute right thing to the right person in the right moment, and an opportunity we didn't expect reveals itself, like a new job or how to fix something or something we really, really needed to know, but didn't know where to look for. Miracles come in every form and size. Don't be so busy looking for the big ones that you miss the little ones all around you!

When we have resisted ourselves long enough, the very change that we have resisted comes anyway and sometimes in a much more difficult way than if we had been more open to differences in our lives earlier. Some part of us deep down is screaming for our lives to be more colorful, complete, and fulfilled. As we talked about earlier, Creation is listening, and it brings us exactly what we request, even when we don't expect it.

For example: Day after day we go to the same job, hating it. We are bored, unfulfilled, and unchallenged, and yet every morning we get up and go again. After all, we need that money, right? We do the bare minimum to get through the day or conversely work way too hard in order to please the boss because that gives us value, right? *(Wrong!)*

One morning we get to work, and as we walk through the office, people step back like the Red Sea being parted by Moses. Through the chasm of people, we see the boss standing there waiting for us. Uh oh.

The boss tells us that our services are no longer needed. No muss no fuss, just pack up and go on home. Shocked, devastated, hurt, we pack our box or two and head to the car. We put the boxes in the backseat and get into the driver's seat. Confusion sets in. Where do we go now? What are we going to do? Oh God, *now what?*

There are a lot of us who, in that moment, would go home and have a humongous pity party. Our livelihood is lost. We might even panic.

But there is another way to handle this. First of all, it is to know that there is a reason for everything and for everything there is a reason. Let's admit it. We were bored, unsatisfied, and unchallenged. We really wanted something different. We got it.

So let's take a ride. As we go down the road, we come to a stoplight. Something inside of us says to turn right. What the heck, we aren't on the clock anymore. OK, let's turn. As we go down the lane, a ball rolls out in front of us, followed by a very excited pooch. We hit the brakes and come to a stop just as the dog runs in front of us. We stop just short of flattening the dog. Darn dog!

While we are sitting there, waiting for our heart to slow down and the dog and his ball to leave the road, a man walks up and thanks us for stopping. "Sorry buddy. He got out the door faster than I could stop him." Right about then he notices the boxes in the backseat. "Hey, are you moving?"

"No, I just got laid off from my job. I don't know what I am going to do now."

"Well, what kind of work do you do?"

Now here is a pivotal moment. Do we say what we were doing or what we really want to do?

Absolutely hands down what we *want*.

"Well, I *was* repairing computers, but the truth is that over all of these years I have had some outstanding ideas for products that would enhance the computer industry by a long shot. I have even built some prototypes. This is my passion, and one day I hope to put my creative ideas to work."

The man gets a peculiar look on his face and briefly pauses. Then he sticks his hand out and says, "Hi. I am Peter Gabriel (pseudonym), CEO of CreativeElectronics.com. You know, we have a place in our company for innovative people like you. Why don't you come by the office, say around two this afternoon and we will talk? If, of course, you are interested . . ."

At two we go to the office to meet Mr. Gabriel, and he shows us around. The entire place is a plethora of creative ideas in motion. The environment is nothing like we have ever seen—bright, cheerful, *comfortable.*

Long story short, Mr. Gabriel, offers us a job at three times our previous pay with twice the benefits and an open schedule in which we can come and go as necessary. He pays to move us to a different state and enough of a sign-on bonus to buy a new home there.

Not only that, but soon after we begin our new job, we become so creative and successful with our ideas that we are put in charge of creative ideas and the technicians who build the prototypes! We win best-of-show for new products at the Mac fair our first year!

This story may seem like a fairy tale, but it is a slightly embellished version of one that actually happened to one of my clients. Magic happens when we are open to the infinite possibilities that are available to us. Change can carry us to the door of an entirely new life experience. The key is that we have to be willing to walk through that door when it opens.

Sometimes we open those doors without realizing what we are doing. On other occasions we intentionally open up opportunities for positive change in our lives merely by being totally present in a now, noticing some subtle clue that an opportunity is at hand, and going for it. How we embrace that opportunity doesn't matter. What matters is that we do! We just have to be willing to step forward into new territory.

With change come challenges. Of course, like anything else, change comes in degrees. Part of why we see change as so difficult is because we look at the whole picture or set of circumstances as if we have to deal with everything all at once. Remember that

everything complex is made up of definable small parts,
each of which is simple.

And besides,

nothing within you ever changes without your participation.

I remember when I was small and worried about something that, to a kid, seemed like a huge dilemma, my dad would ask me how to eat an elephant. My mind would go directly to the size and weight of the beast and even the toughness of the skin of an elephant. (Could my small teeth even bite it?) In my imagination the elephant was covered in mud—way too dirty to eat! About then Dad would laugh and say "You eat an elephant one bite at a time, of course!"

Change is like the elephant. Change can seem overwhelming, but if we find ourselves immersed in the unknown, all we need to do is begin to unravel the complexity to define the simplicities.

Simplicities are our lifelines in any set of circumstances.

The simplicities become a trail, a map from one moment to the next. One by one, they unfold to a greater and greater understanding of any experience.

In other words, we often become so overwhelmed by the immensity of a situation that we fail to see that if we just deal with one aspect at a time, before you know it, we have surmounted the entire situation!

For instance, when I was a real estate broker, I volunteered to be in charge of the annual Board of Realtors Christmas banquet. It was a much bigger deal than I had realized. It involved planning menus, getting decorations, renting a place to have the event; it had little to no budget, and it required entertainment, a sound system, bar staff, and a whole lot more. When I first sat down to begin putting the event together, I was overwhelmed. It was vastly out of my realm of experience. Being a visionary, I tend to see things completed, not all of the little details that get you there. In fact, I abhor details.

The first thing to do was to separate out all of the parts to the event. So I made an outline. To get this, we need that. OK, now what? Well, I thought, the next thing to do was to find a place that specialized in that kind of event and that could help with the details (the food, décor, staffing, and so on). So I did. I went over the menus with the facility staff, and I told them how I envisioned the room being set up from what I knew would be happening at the banquet. They decorated around my plans. Because this event was for such a diverse group of people, I chose more than one kind of entertainment. First I chose one that everyone would participate in. With the assistance of another Realtor, I wrote a simple, hilarious play, and we gave everyone their lines to the play as they came in the door. No one knew what came before or after their given lines. It was too funny. We also hired a DJ, who brought a wide variety of music and was open to requests. Yes, you *can* please *almost* everyone! The establishment provided bartenders for an extra fee. In order to keep costs down, we required all attendees to bring their own bottles and leave their bottle at the bar with their name on it. On and on, one part of the puzzle at a time was solved, until the resulting gala was a smashing success! When it was completed, that elephant didn't look so big at all, and we were all quite full!

What we don't often realize is that all change comes from within. It is not something that happens to us. It is something that on some level we require for the expansion of our soul's experience.

No matter what we say, or what we do or do not do, some part of us deep inside is screaming for us to do something different. Are we listening?

When our children see us move into change with grace and ease, they learn elasticity. They learn to go with the flow and not to be ruffled by what comes along and by changes in their direction. They learn to embrace those moments of opportunity and to be carried into magnificent moments of new discovery.

Exercise: Make a Change Now

Think of one thing that you really want to change in your life. It doesn't have to be the most major change on your list (unless you want it to be). Choose something that for a long time you have said "if only" or "one day I am going to ..."

Whatever change you choose, make sure that it will take you out of your comfort zone. It can be as easy as changing the hairstyle you have worn for years or the color of your clothes. It can be to rearrange a room that has been the same forever, ending or beginning a relationship, moving house, or reacting to certain people in a new way. Start with something small if necessary.

Oh! Feel that resistance to making it happen? Are the excuses on autopilot, telling you all of the reasons that you shouldn't change anything? Those excuses are lies that are born of fear.

Even if you don't have a plan, make that change! Do so without any expectations and know that whatever it is, it will be perfect in its outcome.

Oh, and never look back. What was, has been. You aren't there anymore, remember? The time is *now!* Go for it!

Exercise with Your Child

Like us, our children become creatures of habit mostly based upon the routine we have or the habits we utilize in our everyday lives. A predictable life can become boring very quickly! Think of fun ways to change what you do in the time that you spend with your child. This can be as easy as taking a different route to school or soccer practice. Or changing where you eat or what you do when everyone in your family is at home. Perhaps you can rearrange your child's room (with their input, of course), or if you make the same meals on the same days, shake it up and make something different. If you usually go to the movies on Friday night, take them to do something more interactive, where you can have good quality time. Make changes regularly. It can be fun.

As you make each change, talk with your child about it. How do they feel about it? Do they have any suggestions about how the change will affect them or everyone? Do they see any opportunities available now that they are doing something differently? Ask them to suggest more changes. You may be surprised at what they come up with!

10

TRUST THAT YOUR RELATIONSHIPS HAVE PURPOSE

Even when it isn't obvious!

Our relationships and the dynamics within them are a direct reflection of who we are inside.

Ouch! That statement may hurt, but it is the truth. All of our relationships mirror to us something about ourselves. Typically we want to blame the other person for the failure or discomfort within our relationships, but the truth is that on some level we are getting exactly what we sought. If we find ourselves fighting to see our value in our relationships, always feeling betrayed or left out, we might consider that we haven't acknowledged our value from the inside out.

How many relationships have *you* had? Have they worked out? If not, why not? What were you looking for in the other person or people? Did not getting it bring you to another, and perhaps even others, so that you were just repeating the same situation with different faces?

What are we looking for? With family? Friends? Lovers? Mates? Why are we not finding it? What kind of dynamics do we bring to our relationships that jeopardize the outcome?

Most of us get into relationships with an agenda. We may not even be aware of what that agenda is, but there it is running our show from the background.

Our neediness—stemming from a a sense of insecurity, emotional emptiness, or even sexual desire—puts us in a position of vulnerability that ultimately gets us into trouble. At the very least we become disappointed that our counterparts just don't seem to give us what we need. The truth is that we looked to them to give us what we thought we didn't have. How could they possibly know what that is if we can't find and acknowledge the lack of it within ourselves? Isn't it time to be finished with neediness? Aren't we ready to embark on entirely new relationship experiences?

Relationships have many faces, but honestly, can all be approached from the same perspective? When we look to another to fill something in us, we have some kind of expectations of what that fulfillment will look like or feel like. As we look to someone else for fulfillment, we lay the potential of our happiness into the laps of our counterparts. *What if* we tried a new approach, like letting everyone, including ourselves, off the hook?

The real secret to a healthy relationship of any kind is to realize that no one has what we are looking for except us.

If we don't value ourselves, recognizing that we are whole and perfect beings just as we are, who else is going to give us that value? We cannot accept from others what we can't recognize in ourselves!

Valuing ourselves goes back to acknowledging our perfection. Some may say that recognizing our perfection and hence valuing ourselves is impossible because others have criticized us for not doing enough or being enough, and thus have taught us to loathe our imperfection. But honestly, those people are passing judgment from their own senses of lack or need.

If we can have relationships that allow for everyone to be who they are, without judgment or fear of reprisal, then we can relax and embrace life to its fullest potential.

Why Love Is Not Like a Hallmark Card

If we go about life thinking that real love is like that depicted in greeting cards and romanticized commercials, what we get are surface relationships that have no depth or long-term chance for survival. Why? Because most cards, most love songs, most anything related to love that is advertised commercially paints a codependent picture of romance. In other words, "I can't live without you." They leave little to no room for the sacredness of self. That is not to say that romance isn't a wonderful thing. It surely is! But let's get real about it.

When we are able to love ourselves unconditionally, accepting ourselves as we are and who we are no matter what, we find inner peace like nothing we have ever experienced. As we find that peace, we begin to emanate it to everyone around us. We have a glow about us that is irresistible to others. People gravitate to us like moths to a flame. We are a flame, bright with the secrets of life.

Our vulnerabilities, which are our fears and previous experiences from which our fears originated, hide in our subconscious and dictate how we react to any given situation. Like the exercise we did in chapter 3, when we have accepted our fears, we are no longer vulnerable to being hurt by others. Our guard is then down, and we become authentic in our relations.

As we learn to become authentic, there is nothing to cover up. Our secrets become moot, and we can be at ease anytime, anywhere with anyone. We become unconditional.

Being unconditional means that we not only accept ourselves for who we are, but we accept everyone else for who they are as well. We become more aware of the motivations of others—what they really mean and even why they mean it. We are off the hook, and so are they.

When we find this kind of freedom, we are able to experience our feelings at very deep levels because we are no longer hiding from them. And because we are able to feel so deeply, we also become able to give our love more freely. No more withholding. No more guarding our perceived perfections and pain. Only purity of relations on authentic levels.

This is true love. First loving the self, and then loving others, becomes unconditional and can be done with ease and grace. The freedom of this is incomparable.

Real love is not a romantic idealistic fantasy. It is a state of being. When we love ourselves, and we live each moment from that complete self-acceptance, others love us back. When we love ourselves, we find it much easier to have compassion for others. In fact, when we *are* love, we are able to see ourselves in the eyes of everyone we meet. When we find unconditionality in ourselves, we are able to see much more clearly because nothing is a threat to us, and those things that we previously saw as challenges now appear to be opportunities!

Finding Fulfillment from the Inside Out

Finding fulfillment on our own isn't really that hard. It begins with self-acknowledgment. Fulfillment from the inside out is nothing more than changing our perception of self. When we do, the entire world looks different to us. Gone are the negativities that haunted our days. Gone is the pain of victimhood. Gone is the angst over if or when we will be loved. What is left is the opportunity for pure joy in life.

As you read this, I imagine at this point you are saying "Yes, but . . ." Or "What if so-and-so won't go along with this new me?" Or "That sounds way to hard." Or "My relationship may not be perfect, but . . ."

There are any number of defensive responses you may have to this information. Look at them. These are part of your defense filters that keep you rooted in place, unable to move forward into greater and different relationships.

Taking responsibility for our experiences and removing the blame from others is a huge step toward having what we want. Typically we tend to want to blame others for not being who or what we thought we had in them. The truth is that those people did the best they could—or not. The point is that it really doesn't matter. The question is, did we do the best we could, and did we learn anything? Or are we going to choose to suffer, wallowing in our pain, carrying that previous relationship around like a dead animal?

When we cart the past around with us, we leave no room for what we really want now.

Worse, we inflict our pain from previous experiences onto the next unsuspecting victim that we befriend or fall in love with, treating them as if they are the one who injured us in the first place. How on earth is this new person supposed to stand a chance? The child within us is mad, hurt, frustrated, and looking for someone to fix us and make it right.

It ain't gonna happen. First of all, no one is a mind reader. How can the new person possibly know what's up when they weren't there previously and so aren't even aware of the experience that we had? They can't! Yet we expect that either they will fix what is broken or they will fill the perceived gap that we think someone else left in us. And that gap is filled with pain. There is no room for anything else and no way to experience unconditionality, that is for sure!

The truth is that the pain is our chosen path. If we want
something different, all we have to do is choose differently.

But first we have to get right with ourselves. Let's admit our part of our experiences. After all, they are our experiences. We chose, we reacted, and we acted. Now let's get real and get into a healthier mode.

There Are No Mistakes

People come together for great purposes. Sometimes we know why, but more often than not we never know. In fact, coming together is perfection personified.

I used to say that the reason that relationships didn't succeed was that people just didn't try hard enough. What I have learned—what I know—is that often relationships end because people *do try too hard,* for whatever reason. They do so from within their private agenda, which isn't always on the forefront of their awareness.

Sometimes though, relationships just run their course and finish. Sometimes they finish with grace and ease, but more often they end with one or more of the participants being hurt and or angry. But there aren't any mistakes in why or how we come together with others.

In the scheme of things, we are part of an intricate weaving of souls, having simple yet complex relations with others as we are infinitely choreographed to do. Sometimes a relationship is a flash in the pan. Others are for lifetimes. Each has purpose and opportunity, and it is up to us what we do with that.

Sometimes relationships are Karmic. This word is really overused, but in this case it is highly applicable. There are things that we can do together with the other person that we couldn't accomplish for ourselves. We harmonize in a perfect creation of relationship and events. With the energy and aid of another person, things set up perfectly for us to accomplish life lessons or growth or even setbacks (as we see them), so that we can become more aware within the journey of our souls. At the same time, we are contributing to the journey of the other person as well.

There comes a time in Karmic relationships when these influences are finished and the reasons for the relationship are completed. In this type of situation, the relationship decays and separation occurs. It is a universal happening. No one is right or wrong. Simply put, the job is done, so we go on to what is next. It doesn't mean that the relationship wasn't important or was less valuable than others. In fact, Karmic relationships can be some of the most powerful and satisfying or challenging that we can have while we are having them.

Our greatest love, whether or not we are still with them, was no mistake. No matter how it turned out, that love took us to our first human depths and heights of loving another person in such a way. We know what that feels like and don't have to grieve it if it is gone; we need to know only that we are capable of feeling great love at *anytime.*

Our most painful relationship wasn't an error of God or anyone else either. It was an opportunity for us to expand to new and different awareness, and to make different choices than we had before. Unfortunately, perhaps, part of that learning curve didn't feel so good because instead of getting the message, we resisted, thinking that the other person had something we needed, and the relationship became so dysfunctional that it was very painful. The question remains: did we get the message, or are we still going to have to have the lesson again and again until we learn something different?

If we are open and choose to see, every one of our relationships teaches us something. The real question is, are we ready to learn? Or do we just want to feel sorry for ourselves because we don't think we got what we wanted or needed? Our painful relationships are generally caused by us fighting against our own fears or projecting our needs onto someone else, who can't possibly fulfill what they don't understand. Or maybe we and they are simply mismatched for whatever reasons got us there in the first place. Often we attract exactly the person we need so that we can choose to change a path of behavior or learn to greater depths, but we don't see it that way. We make the pain all the other person's fault, no matter what the challenge!

Painful relationships, when there is arguing, dissonance, or other seemingly negative forces at work, are simply opportunities for us to become aware of our vulnerabilities so that we can grow into healthier relationships, mostly within ourselves. If we were to look back to those relationships from a completely honest perspective, we would find that we railed and kicked and screamed to stay in the relationship even though it offered little of what we thought we needed at the time. We stayed because of some subconscious sense of need. We stayed because we feared the unknown possibilities of doing something different. We stayed in our comfortable discomfort.

We do resist change.

We often opt to stay in comfortable discomfort because the unknown scares us. But then being with someone who does not honor us, who uses or, worse, abuses us, is not OK. Really. Not. OK.

The thing to do is recognize in ourselves just why that experience has been perfect. When we look at the situation honestly and we don't like what we see, we might also ask ourselves why we are still there.

We have to leave the other person out of it for a minute. What the heck are we doing? What untruths are we accepting in our own reckoning that cause us to stay in relationships that are so not good for us or the other person? Once we realize the answers to these questions, our path becomes clear, if we let it. And the relief of being free from the discomfort can be profound, and the self-discovery is priceless.

Sometimes partners just grow in different directions. Conversely, often one partner embraces life and grows tremendously while the other maintains the status quo, not seeming to need or seek change or expansion. Changes in the relationship begin to occur subtly, until one day the two people seem to have nothing in common at all.

The important thing to remember is that if a relationship has run its course, and you honestly feel that working together (if both parties are willing to do so) won't change what is needed, it is OK to move on in life and sever the relationship.

Social morals and mores in the past have dictated that once two people are together, they are always together. These types of social and personal expectations cause great amounts of frustration and disharmony in couples whose relationship has truly run its course. Sometimes these social pressures cause couples to settle for each other, leaving in each of them a great chasm of emptiness for what they never experienced.

It is better to admit that the relationship is over than to torture each other indefinitely. There is nothing wrong at all about ending a relationship that has finished. Ending a relationship does not have to be a negative experience, nor does the relationship need to be considered a failure. Finishing relationships is simply part of life. If happiness is no longer available in the relationship, staying in a relationship is destructive to both people over the long term. No one has to be angry or mad. Relationships can end from the heart, responsibly and unthreatening to both parties. After all, there was a lot of good in the relationship, right? You got together for some reason, right? Why dishonor that?

The question is, did you learn anything? Are you being honest with yourself about what the relationship brought, or are you continuing to deny, deny, deny?

To have relationships that are in truth, and that have any chance of being fulfilling and of great depth, we must have a great relationship with ourselves first. We must love ourselves from our toenails up and to the depths of our very souls. We have to value ourselves beyond measure. We must be willing to see the truth of every situation in which we find ourselves, and we must be willing to stand in that truth, telling it with love both to ourselves and to our partner. We must never, ever believe that anyone has more power than we do, and we must be willing to expose our inner selves, our most vulnerable selves, to the essence of love. Otherwise all of our relationships will be on the surface. We will always be defensive and feel that we are lacking.

Remember, no one can love you like you can, but they can come close if you give them a chance! When you are ready to expose yourself fully, first to yourself and then to another, you will attract someone who shares exactly what you are looking to find!

Exercise: What Kind of Relationship Do I Want?

Take yourself to a quiet, comfortable place to sit. At your leisure, examine the following questions honestly with yourself. Even if you are already in a relationship, you may discover inner perceptions that are enhancing or interfering with your relationship.

- What am I looking for in my lover (spouse, significant other, partner—whatever applies)? What kind of traits am I looking for in someone else? Do I have those traits? Do I use them?

- What do I feel is missing in me that my partner can give? Why do I really feel like it is missing? Can I remember when I first felt that way? What happened then? Is how I feel now really because I feel like something is missing, or is it because I developed a perception the first time I felt like this? How can I feel full and whole without looking to someone else to fill my perceived gaps?

- Do I really need someone in my life? If so, why? If not, why not?

- What do I have to give to a relationship? What about me would attract another person?

- Am I really willing to receive the love I want? Do I know how? If I feel funny about receiving, how will I ever have the full relationship I want? Am I willing to be open to my value?

- Am I willing to communicate openly with my partner and share an equal relationship?

Exercise with Your Child

Teaching children about relationships can be done by example. When good healthy relationship dynamics are established in the parents or caregivers, the children experience healthfulness in their environments. But what about when they are in school or among their peers?

Have a discussion with your child about the kinds of traits that we want in our friends and the people that we choose to have around us. Emphasize that friends and relationships are always a choice and that decisions can be remade at any time. Children often feel pressured to belong and may choose their friends accordingly. Make sure that your child knows that it is OK to be who they are and that no other person changes that.

11

CARRY YOUR OWN BAGGAGE

It's too heavy for me!

How involved do we get in the pain of others because we feel sorry for them or are under the illusion that we can fix what is broken?

Many times relationships have a hero and a victim. The victim carries their past experiences like a badge of merit and an excuse for every poor behavior that they exhibit. The hero takes the position of caretaker to gain a perception of value. The hero creates a prison by being the responsible party, while the victim suffers in the prison by choosing to be there. So two sets of dynamics fall into a very dysfunctional pattern: the victim is enabled by the hero, and the hero is enabled by the victim. And no one really wins.

While in a way this match might seem to be made in heaven, the problem is that it stunts the further development of either partner.

The partner who perceives themselves as damaged doesn't move past the bonds of pain. Clearly, the pain is exacerbated by the need to be taken care of. Seeing one's self as needy validates the perception of being incapable or not enough. The victim's self-worth is fairly nonexistent, and their self-image is not pretty. Since their needs are being met by someone else, they don't need to make a real effort to see themselves as well, whole, and strong. So the victim will remain in a state of perceived weakness or victimhood.

The hero, on the other hand, gains a false sense of power by being in charge, even in control. An underlying sense of dominance is exacerbated by the partner's apparent weakness. Knowing only how to give, the hero hasn't learned to receive and generally blocks any personal needs in order to gain a sense of importance. The hero doesn't usually know how to fully display or share on an emotional level because they are unable to make a full heart connection with their partner.

In this kind of situation, balance is nearly impossible to maintain, and there is little to no growth or expansion by either party.

Communication

Relationships are like Jello. When the environment is cool, Jello is resilient and bounces back to its original shape. When the environment is too hot, the Jell-O quickly dissolves into an unrecognizable sticky mess.

Our environment gets hot when we don't communicate our inner feelings, needs, wants, desires, likes and dislikes, or fears. When we keep everything in, no one has a clue who we really are or what we feel. Good communication is paramount to a healthy, balanced relationship. Too often we keep our mouths shut, not telling anyone anything deep or too important about ourselves, because it feels unsafe. We become vulnerable when we expose ourselves, making ourselves subject to having information used against us, to inflict more pain than we already had.

The fact is that in that moment we have given someone else more value than we give ourselves. By not speaking

up, we tacitly say that someone else's wishes or needs are
far more important than ours. This is a lie!

When we give our power to others, at some point, natural selection will seek balance. But by then we will have lost our confidence and our *joie de vivre* and withered into unhappiness, or we will have settled for our lot in life.

Living an unhappy, unfulfilled life is not what we came to
earth to do! We have come here to embrace our lives and
live them fully and joyously!

If we have truly reckoned with ourselves and become honest inside of ourselves, feelings of lacking safety dissipate, and we are left with solid ground to stand on.

Remember, learning to tell the truth can be difficult at first, but becomes easier the more we do it. It is as simple as telling one truth at a time, gaining confidence each time, and then telling the truth more until that is all there is.

As mentioned in chapter 1, the main thing to remember is that

the message is always dependent upon its delivery.

How we say what we mean has everything to do with how we are heard. If we speak from a perspective of defense, we will meet opposition from others. If we speak with love and acceptance, then we will receive loving acceptance back. (If we don't, we might want to consider who we are with and why.) If we speak with integrity, we have said our truth and offered it to be heard. If it is heard, then so it is. If not, then so it is. How others react to our truth says a lot about our relationships with them.

If what we have to say is considered and responded to in like fashion, then we know that we have a caring, honest relationship. If our feelings, wants, needs, opinions, or anything else are being battled, then we know that we are not being heard and, because of that, we are also not being honored.

Of course, we must communicate thoughtfully and without an agenda. We must make sure that our communications express our internal views and that we are not projecting our feelings and fears onto the other person. Sometimes when we haven't taken the time or don't have the awareness to know what we really feel, we try to make others responsible for our baggage. This is also not acceptable, and yet it is extremely common.

We must be self-aware enough that we can talk about our internal stuff without any attempt to make another person responsible for what is our doing alone.

We really have to own our stuff. Once we have done so, we become able to communicate with clarity.

In tandem with clear, honest communication come good listening skills. If we are so busy formulating our next defense or opinion, barely able to keep it in until it is our turn to speak, we aren't hearing the response we requested in the first place.

When we are uncomfortable in a situation, one of the first responses our body has is to stop breathing for a moment. When we do hold our breath, our energy temporarily stops flowing, and the inside of our bodies becomes tense. Our emotions create a biological cycle, and as we continue to emote, chemical and electrical responses cause the cycle to intensify. This cycle of biological and emotional events strongly affects our response to the stimuli. So instead, breathe, relax, and listen to what is being said in response to your words.

Another part of solid communication is eye contact. When we speak to another, or interact in any way, we must look at them directly. Looking into another's eyes says that we are present, interested, intentional, and on equal ground with the other person. The eyes also speak to the other on levels where there are no words.

When we connect eye to eye with another, the divine in each of us can be recognized.

And when the divine is recognized, communication is clear. Of course, we need to say what we mean. It is easy to look at the floor, or more subtly, position our bodies in opposition to our words. Everything must match. And, of course, our actions must correspond to our words. If we say something, then we must do or be that, whatever the case may be. One clear sign that someone isn't being honest is that their words and actions don't match. They might say one thing, but then exhibit another via their behaviors. This mismatch is a sure indication that someone is only saying the words that they think want to be heard. Ultimately, they will go on to do what they want anyway, exhibiting no real change.

Our words, our actions, our thoughts, our heart of hearts—all must be in alliance with the sentiments we are sharing.

The Dynamics: Unresolved Issues

The dynamics of relations between human beings are intricate. When two or more lives blend, their stories can become entangled, streamlined, competitive, or synergistic as the details of the stories begin to unfold. Certain dynamics, such as intimacy, good communication techniques, honesty, honor, and good intentions, are healthy and desirable. But other dynamics can ruin or destroy relationships.

Control Issues

Control issues are one of the foremost dynamics in relationships. One or both parties have an inner need to know what is coming next and to make sure that everything happens according to those expectations. Because of this need, each party utilizes certain tactics in order to maintain a sense of control. A few of the more common modalities used for control are:

Withholding Affection: Affection is withheld as punishment until the controlling person gets his or her way. This withholding is cruel and unnecessary. Affection between people, whether they are in a friendship or a bonded love relationship, is vital to the balance and satisfaction of the relationship. Intimacy is a great part of the closeness people feel together. When one withholds affection, it denotes selfishness and a lack of trust. Further, withholding is a statement of higher value, meaning that the controlling partner is making a stand for dominance. This is not OK.

Subtleties: Subtleties are inferences or indirect remarks or behaviors that imply an outcome and are used to create doubt. Subtleties usually are directly related to manipulation. Manipulation of another often involves demeaning them for being who they are. That is not healthy. Manipulation is about not being honest enough with the self and thus finding gentle authentic power, and instead gaining false power by belittling another by indirect nuances, manipulation, or direct comments. In any relationship *this is not acceptable!*

Direct communication is necessary for clear understanding and for the confidence of both parties. The more one is undermined, the more they are likely to begin to keep secrets and lose a sense of self, placing their power in the hands of the other. This is destructive and ultimately causes the controlling party to lose respect for the other.

Criticism: Criticism is used to undermine the confidence of the receiving person, and is generally used when the one doing the criticizing has low self-esteem or is insecure. Criticism gives the critic a false sense of power. It is unfair and unnecessary because both parties are entitled to be who they are in spite of their differences.

Rage: Rage is used to intimidate and gain a perception of power. Rage coming from an adult human being can be terrifying, and usually we avoid rage-filled confrontations at all costs. When rage is used against someone, it is not usually even about what is going on in the moment, but a deeper unacknowledged set of issues from the past. People who rage do not usually face their own issues and gain a false sense of power by bullying others with their explosions. Trying to reason with someone who is raging is generally impossible if the current experience is being addressed. Instead, it is best to understand the background and cause of the insecurity that causes the rage in the first place. Fighting back with someone who is raging can be dangerous and will not stop it. In fact, fighting with someone who is raging will often incite them even further.

Jealousy: Jealousy is one of the most manipulative forms of control. It is generally unfounded and is used to keep a partner close at hand. Jealousy comes from fear of loss, abandonment, rejection, or something else. It is completely fear based and at times even irrational. Jealousy is used to control who one sees or what one does, when, and for how long.

Another aspect of jealousy is projection. Perhaps the jealous partner has their own thoughts of straying to another or others outside of the relationship and is projecting those thoughts onto an innocent partner.

A good sense of trust cannot be developed when jealousy is ruling the nest. Jealousy is destructive and can have opposite results. A partner may begin to feel that since they are not trusted, seeking fulfillment or even relief from the accusations of the jealous partner, they might become involved on some level with another person or persons.

Ultimately, jealousy can cause the original imaginary scenario to become a reality.

Overall, control issues are highly destructive and create huge dysfunction in a relationship.

Other Destructive Dynamics

Adult-Child Behavior: In our psyche there is a child who remains, for whatever reasons, spoiled or feels as if it is lacking in basic attention and needs. This child often acts out in our adult relationships when it doesn't get what it wants. Coming through an adult body, this child can be daunting, terrifying, or simply a royal pain.

When we act from our child self, we are not taking responsibility for our actions. We expect someone else to fix what we think is wrong or give us what we need. We throw intimidating fits or perhaps even pick a fight. Some adult children break things or act abusively toward their partners. *This is completely and equivocally not acceptable.*

The dysfunctional adult child operates from a dark place of need, or from a place of having been catered to as a child, and doesn't quite understand adult dynamics. To the adult child, everything that happens is someone else's fault. They find it impossible to own their own stuff. The best way to deal with their behavior is to be a loving mirror for them. A mirror—not a parent.

It is easy to fall into a parent role in response to this kind of behavior. Of course, acting like a parent is the worst thing we could do because it encourages the adult child to act out even more. Arguing gets you nowhere because, at least subconsciously, the adult child has figured out every answer to every objection long before pitching that fit. Instead, it is best simply not to play that game. The child within the adult must learn that being an adult doesn't involve acting out or creating scenes.

The important thing to do is, if possible, to get to the root of the issue. What is it about the situation that brought that child forward in the first place? Was the other person simply not getting their way, or is the situation actually related to something that happened in their childhood? Is this a habitual behavior? What current need isn't being met, at least in that person's perception? What are they afraid of, and how can that fear be allayed? How can that person give to themselves what they need without all the fuss?

Was some of this behavior the result of child abuse or sexual abuse? If so, then, first of all, the abuse can't be used as an excuse. Rather, the victim must work through the emotions of the abuse in a healthy and responsible way and, if necessary, with professional help. One does not need to relive past abuse or the pain of it to move beyond the abuse. Doing so simply requires finding a current sense of safety, which isn't always easy, but is possible!

Whatever the case, the inner child must learn skills that will enable them to learn to behave acceptably. Instead of reacting and fighting back when the child is in action with your partner, it is best to just not participate at all until the adult shows back up and is willing to talk responsibly.

Narcissism: Narcissism is another very frustrating behavior. A narcissist lives their life on the inside, keeping everything in, rarely and barely exposing their thoughts and feelings to others. This behavior makes it impossible to reason with them, because when you do get communication, it is generally only their bottom line. Or they start in the middle of their reasoning process, and you never have any idea about how they got to that point, what affected them, or what triggered them.

By the time you experience their behavior, it may seem very disconnected to what is currently happening, appearing to make little or no sense to the current situation. The narcissist's entire world is inside of them, and getting a glimpse is often painful. After all, they have internalized because they either don't have the life skills to make themselves feel safe when they are exposed, or they have so much pain from previous circumstances that they became bogged down, not knowing how to process that pain and never dealing with it at all.

To work better with someone narcissistic, open communication is encouraged. Ask pointed questions that are not attached to your hurt emotions. Get the other person to explain more thoroughly what they mean and why. Explaining is difficult for them, so patience is definitely a virtue.

Narcissistic behavior isn't about you at all. It is about the narcissist's inability to bring forward what is within.

On the flip side, narcissistic behavior can also be a manipulative tool. On some level the narcissist feels as if the less you know, the better. They feel more powerful within their secrets. Withholding information keeps the narcissist's partner off balance enough that they become insecure and desperate for attention.

Projection: Projecting our feelings onto another person can cause us a lot of grief. Sometimes, without realizing it, we may actually accuse another person of exactly what we are thinking or feeling. Projection is generally a result of us not being honest with ourselves in the first place.

The truth is that when we start projecting our feelings onto others, we are afraid of or overwhelmed by whatever emotions we haven't yet recognized. If we can step back and take a look at what we are doing with an honest eye, we can realize that we are causing much of the situation ourselves.

Triangles: Triangles are dangerous games to play. Inadvertently, or even habitually, we sometimes add a third person into a relationship we are already having. Often when there is a triangle, it is because we have difficulty committing ourselves to one situation in any depth. Or we need or are looking for something that our partner doesn't bring to the relationship, but another person does very well.

Sometimes we add a third person to distract ourselves, or to dilute or defray the intensity of the relationship, and by doing so we often contribute to the other two participants' feelings of mistrust, jealousy, or downright hurt. Why? Because we are generally being dishonest, if even indirectly.

Further, each person in the triangle needs attention of some kind, and usually one person is trying to balance both of the other people in their life. What happens is jealousy, deceit, secrets, and imbalance all the way around. Triangles can have many facets and come up in most any type of relationships. They are unhealthy and destructive. If you are in a triangle that is uncomfortable, make a choice. If you are worried about getting hurt or hurting someone, know that it is very likely to happen anyway. Separate yourself from the triangle or own your part in it, and be honest with both other parties. If each party is truly that connected with you, and your relationship with each is solid, everything will work out just fine. If not, then the relationships weren't founded in truth anyway.

This pattern is likely to be repeated more than once in your life. You can have what you need without closing yourself into this type of dynamic. You are too valuable to make yourself a pawn in a game of imbalance.

Compromising Yourself: Compromising yourself in a relationship can be deadly to both the relationship and your self-esteem. Compromising yourself is not the same as compromising on a specific issue. It is giving up your values, your dreams, wants, needs, desires, and anything else you can think of, in deference to another person. Giving up yourself leaves you powerless, out of control, and ultimately looking up one day and wondering where your hopes and dreams went and how to find yourself again.

Maintaining a sense of self is vital to sustaining yourself in a spiritual, mental, and physical way.

No one has the right or the power to expect you to be anything but who you are—no matter what.

If someone expects you to be anything but who you are, look at the relationship closely. Is it one you really want to be in?

Often when we stay in relationships that are not to our best interest, we do so because we are addicted to the dynamics that are going on. Think about it. Think about relationships that you no longer have. When you think of that person, what do you miss? Usually it is the things that made you crazy in the first place.

We often hold on to relationships out of a sense of desperation, feeling that the unknown is worse than our comfortable discomfort. Sometimes it is best to just bite the bullet and leap into the chasm of the unknown.

If you find yourself doing nothing but complaining about your relationship to your partner or others and that nothing ever really changes, chances are that you are living an addiction. The negative aspects of the relationship become tools for getting attention at the expense of your relationship and your partner.

If this is the case for you, what is it that you need, and what positive steps can you take to get it in a more healthy way? Let go of the negative, even if it means being alone for a while. Get yourself together. Take time to get to know yourself. Your partner can never give you whatever it is that is causing you to seek attention in this way.

Exercise: Turning Things Around

Think of one thing in your current relationship that really bothers you. If you are not in a current relationship, think of one thing in a previous relationship that bothered you. Behaviors, habits, ways of saying things, parts of people's bodies, the way they eat or dress, whatever—these can all be things that really get on our nerves.

Take a closer look at that one thing (even if there are or were many to choose from), and ask yourself why it bothers you so much. Is it that you feel that your partner's behavior may reflect directly on you? Do you react because, as a child, you were punished for doing that same thing?

For instance, when I was small, if I left a drawer or cabinet open or a chair pulled away from the dining table, I was corrected for doing so and even sometimes spanked. To this day I am hypervigilant about keeping cabinets and drawers closed and pushing my chair up to the table. When my husband leaves the cabinets open, as he often does, I sometimes react internally and initially with a flash of anger. And then I realize that, oh, I don't have to worry about that anymore, and it is really OK if he leaves the cabinets open!

The point is to become aware of why you judge another's behaviors in the way that you do. If the behavior is truly rude, inconsiderate, or even unacceptable, you can address it accordingly with your partner.

Exercise with Your Child

Every kid comes home and says, "I don't like so-and-so because he or she is . . . ." When your child does this, help them become aware why they don't like that person. Usually someone else said it first, and, taking the comment as truth, your child is simply parroting it. Help them look further into the situation and to create awareness about differences in people and perceptions. If your child doesn't like someone because of a behavior, have them look further to see if they can determine why the other child is acting out in such a way. For instance, often when kids bully others, it is because they are really feeling powerless or someone at home is treating the child in an aggressive or abusive way. Some kids are quiet or don't participate much because they don't have self-confidence. Teach your child how to befriend children who may not be exactly like everyone else and how to be compassionate about others. Teach your child that prejudging others is really about themselves, not about the other people or person.

12

DUMP YOUR PARENT ISSUES

Whose relationship are you really living?

Once the wedding rings are in place and the reception is over, it is as if someone has flipped a switch and we settle into becoming our parents. We react to our spouses the way our parents react or reacted to each other. We make decisions based upon what our parents might have done. Often we even take on aspects of our parents' personalities. And all or most of this we do on a subconscious level.

All through our childhoods, we are glaringly and subtly conditioned to learn behaviors that our parents believe are right.

Their examples to us become us, and we embody the presence of our parents even when they are no longer there.

If we really look at our behavioral patterns, we can begin to see our parents in them. What we need to remember is that while many of the values they taught us were good ones, we do have lives of our own and truths that are ours.

We cannot live our lives fully when we are trying to be anything that we think someone else expects.

We are individuals with passions and choices all our own.

To mimic our parents robs us of experiencing our life journeys from within the truth of who we are. In fact, when we do, we quickly lose our sense of self, becoming unhappy and feeling unfulfilled. We begin to strive for something that is truly unobtainable, looking for approval in all the wrong places. We don't need approval. What we need is self-recognition.

Parent issues are some of the worst and most long-standing issues we can have. If we didn't feel nurtured as a child and therefore as an adult, we might look for a mother figure. If we never got enough of or any of our father's attention, we might look for men whom we can look up to and who can give us what we think we need: approval, validation, value.

The truth is, once again, that no one can give us those things but us.

Parent dynamics in a relationship are more common than you might think. They are some of the most difficult to surpass because they are so ingrained. When children do not have what they need, they spend the rest of their life trying to change that. Their attempts can create sets of behaviors and dynamics between people that are frustrating and even painful. The most important advice is not to play into the parent role, which can happen before you realize it.

For instance, a man marries a woman who is very strong, decisive, and powerful. He does not feel that he has these traits because he lacks a strong mother figure. Everything is hunky-dory until the honeymoon is over. Then, when the new wife acts from within her innate power, the very thing he was attracted to in the first place, he throws a fit and does something unacceptable to retaliate. She immediately reprimands him, and before you know it, mother and son are acting together all over again.

Conversely, say a woman didn't get the acknowledgment she felt she needed from her father. Perhaps he worked two jobs or was emotionally inept. Perhaps he left the family when she was a child. Whatever the case, she marries a man just like him and pretty soon is feeling her marriage is lacking. She does things for her husband's approval and sometimes even makes a list of her daily accomplishments in order to be recognized, but she still goes unnoticed and wonders why. She becomes a royal nag, he is pushed farther and farther away, and the marriage frazzles. Her biggest fear of being unnoticed has come to reality—again.

A lot of dynamics can fall into the parent-issue department. A hypochondriac, someone who is always sick, is looking for attention and usually gets it until their counterparts get tired of the game. Someone who is an eternal victim also craves attention and doesn't have the skill to get it in positive form. The same goes for those people who make themselves omnipotent, loud, and always right, while on the inside they are terrified of being wrong.

Whatever the issues or origins, all of them can be overcome with self-honesty and sincere effort to dissociate from habitual patterns. If you recognize any of these patterns in yourself, as an individual or a parent, look to the root cause and deal with the accompanying fears. Once identified, the vulnerabilities and their protracted issues can be alleviated.

The greatest awareness of all is that if we carry any of these issues or others, it is a great possibility that we will inadvertently teach them to our children. Whoever we are is who we teach our children to be. What examples of functionality do we want to share with our children? If we are in denial, so they will be. If we are in pain, so they will be. If we are in truth, so they will be. If we are happy and healthy human beings, so they will be. If we show them.

Becoming aware of and willing to change our habitual and dysfunctional behaviors will assure our children a start in life that is way ahead of the one that we had!

The Bottom Line for Healthy Relationships

If we haven't dealt with our inner issues, we will carry them into every relationship that we have.

We must view our friends, lovers, partners, and others with a sense of equality, honoring and respecting them as we expect them to do for us. We must see ourselves in an equal light to our partner, no matter what.

We have to leave room in any relationship for each party to maintain their personal interests and sense of individuality. We need time to explore our interests, to revitalize our senses of excitement. Ultimately, when each party is free to be who they are, the excitement in a relationship is ongoing. There is more to talk about, and the relationship can expand in its depth at a natural rate. Our sense of self is vital to our functioning and healthfulness. When we lose that, we have no resources from which to work.

We must be willing not only to communicate honestly, but also to listen well. Open and honest communications will alleviate most fears.

Honesty in any relationship is paramount to its success. Once a sense of mistrust develops, the relationship is doomed. Honest is the only way to be.

Fairness and openness to new ideas and circumstances are very important. Being fair and willing to give and take, as long as balance is maintained, is excellent.

A great relationship has passion, not just in the bedroom, but also in life. Excitement for each other often becomes lost in the course of everyday living. Work schedules can get in the way as well. My suggestion is make regular dates with each other and do new and different things. Don't always go to the same places. That gets boring. Plan getaways regularly, if possible, or even try weekends with a theme.

Be willing to gracefully accept for yourself as much as you give. If you don't, you are robbing your partner of the joy of giving to you. Know that you have value that is infinite!

Have no expectations, as they will only serve to set you up for disappointment. Stay in the now, not what was or might be. Be willing to be flexible with your partner. Schedules change, as do interests and focus. Be willing to go with the flow no matter what.

Do not judge your partner in comparison to yourself. You are two different people who came together to complement each other. Judgment begets inequality, and inequality is disastrous to any relationship.

Honor your friends, lovers, family, and children as if they were priceless treasures. They are!

Be *now*. Stay present in all your relationships. Be sensitive to what is happening inside of you and what those in your relationships are experiencing. Be connected.

Be happy! Don't always look for what you don't have. Be now and find the positive in everything around you. Everything that you need is on the inside. No one else can give you what you don't give yourself. Be now. Do what you want. Be a partner, not the enemy. Live your relationship to its fullest potential.

Relationships don't just happen. They blossom with the help of those involved. Sometimes that takes some work, but the results can be far worth it. Be strong when necessary and soft every moment that you can. Stay in your heart, especially when your fears rear up to bite you. Remember that your partner wasn't likely there when those fears were born. Don't make your partner responsible for them!

Love deeply your friends, spouses, lovers, partners, your children. Love with all that you are, but first of all, love yourself just as you are. You are an amazing, perfect, whole human being just as you are!

Exercise: Examining My Motivations for Relationships

Ask yourself what it is that you seek in others. What traits do you look for in your friends and love relationships? Once you have identified the traits in others, ask yourself if you acknowledge the very same ones in yourself. Look at your answers carefully! If you don't recognize these traits within you, look at why. What is it that you feel you need from other people that you don't already have? As you discover each of the traits that you feel you lack, look at various ways that you can apply them to your life experience from your own internal resources. Find ways to use these traits in your life.

Exercise with Your Child

Every child has early issues with their friends. Often children don't understand what causes the behaviors that their friends exhibit, especially when their feelings are hurt. As you learn to recognize relationship dynamics, explain to your child how what someone else has done had nothing to do with your child. Show them how everyone reacts to situations differently and that some people have more skill than others when it comes to how they react. Teach your child how to be compassionate instead of judgmental. Ask your child to find reasons to be compassionate in each situation that they bring to you. Help your child to see the truth beyond the dynamics.

13

HAVE IT ALL

What are you waiting for?

One of my observations stemming from working with such a large sampling of people is that we create our lives from the perspectives that others have given us. We are often conservative in our actual playing out of the creative process because we feel as if what we want is limited to what we should have. Our desires become restricted by old mental tapes of the reward-and-punishment game. If you perform a certain way, then you will be rewarded accordingly.

We teach our children the same kind of perceptions. We tell them that if they are good for an hour, then they can have ice cream or a new toy. We teach them that their behaviors directly reward them. We teach them to be dishonest, behaving for reward rather than because the behavior is appropriate. Many of them behave only when doing so is for their gain. So they learn to be good to get. And then if they don't get, they must not be good or good enough. This belief propagates a lifelong need for instant gratification that can and usually will create a deep sense of lack when the child has grown. The adult will always be seeking what is next rather than being present with what is and appreciating it at face value.

Having what we want or need isn't a luxury—it is our God-given right. As human beings we tend to create our life scenarios based upon a lack of self-worth, feelings about what we deserve or don't, what limitations we see for ourselves, and great expectations that aren't realistic. Or if not these specific things, then these kinds of ideas.

The people who are the greatest success in life have only one secret: they believe.

They believe in the reality they are creating without a doubt and without question. They live as if that reality has already happened, and they don't base the results upon whether or not they deserve it, can have it, or anything else except the power of their imaginings.

Then here we are. We dream. We imagine. We want, desire, and wish, and sometimes our longings become reality, but not usually. Sometimes it seems like we almost get there and then *boom!* Something or a series of somethings stop the progress. *Why is that?* Why is it that the things that we want don't happen? Only lucky people get everything they want, right? *Not!*

The purest process of creation is right here, all of the time. The possibilities are infinite. Can we accept what we want? Do we deserve what we dream? What if someone else doesn't do their part? How can we have anything that we want?

Creation Is a Harmonic Field

If we are going to successfully create the kind of life that we want, to live our dreams and desires, and then pass the secrets of our amazing creative muscle to our children, we must first recognize the power that we have in the creative process.

The success of the film and the book *The Secret* is an indication that millions of people are ready for change in their lives. It is time to take a different approach to how we get what we want or need. When we are ready for change, it is because we are bored, not getting what we want, or needing more challenge in our lives. *The Secret* is telling the truth. What the authors did not explain is how and why the Secret works. Here is the secret to *The Secret:*

Each of us is made up of a set of harmonic frequencies, which in turn are made up of light, color, and sound. This composition is a lot like an intricate musical chord. Every one of us is a unique chord in all of Creation. No two people are harmonized quite the same. That is why we are attracted to some people right away and repelled by others immediately.

The rest of Creation, all matter, is a lot like the lined page on which we draw the chords that create a body of music—in this case, our lives. The page is the glue that holds the symphony of us together. The lines where we put the notes on are communication directions that carry definite messages. We read the music left to right, but Creation senses from every direction at once, seeking along infinite pathways for information about what to do next. In turn, Creation is communicating with us on elaborate levels and giving us everything that we need to know. Because of this, each of us is an intricate and necessary part of all Creation.

Each of us is extremely important, because without every one of us as a part of the entire composition, the symphony can't exist.

Written on a page of musical composition are not only the notes and the chords, but also all of the instructions about how to play each part of the symphony. That includes what instruments to use, the mood, the pace, whether the music is expressed softly or with vigor—all of it.

When we create our own symphony—in this case, how we live our lives—we literally create a set of instructions that describes what we want our lives to be like, how it will feel, what instruments it will take to make it whole, and how beautifully every note will come together as we express our feelings within each progressive life experience. As we write our life symphony, the rest of Creation obliges by bringing to us exactly what we need for the grand performance.

The most wonderful part of our creative process is that we have everything available to us that we could possibly need. The music of everything that came before us is within every cell of our bodies. In addition, the infinite possibilities of our future are resident within us. In any given moment, we can draw upon that information to change what is happening.

Everything that has ever happened anywhere, at any time, is written in the complexity of the harmonics of Creation. All of that information is stored in different frequencies of light. Imagine, the endless entirety of history up to now and the infinite possibilities for the future are contained in an intangible library that we can access any time we choose!

Because we are made of the same stuff as everything else in Creation, we have the memory of everything that has happened inside of us. We have an invisible set of instructions inside of us that helps us choose our life experiences.

More importantly, that same instruction book tells us where to go next, how to get there, and even who we are in relation to everything else in Creation. The information comes to us as intuitive guidance—thoughts from left field that have nothing to do with what else we happen to be thinking in the moment.

We can draw upon the infinite to clarify what we need, want, or desire simply because it is us and we are it. We are unlimited beings of a greater whole, woven as part of an infinite tapestry that is more complex than our thinking minds can grasp. Creation is listening to us 24/7. The question is, are we listening to it?

For the purpose of even greater understanding, imagine that on both the smallest and the grandest levels of existence, Creation is a repetitive pattern of predictable geometric shapes. The basic fabric of Creation is founded upon the octahedron shape, which looks a lot like a ball with eight flat sides on the surface. The octahedron is comprised of eight four-sided pyramids. The pyramids have a system of light and harmonics just like we do. Each individual structure, first the pyramid and then the octahedron, has an individual set of harmonics that is a separate consciousness from all other particles.

As the octahedron-shaped particles come together to change reality into matter, they harmonize based upon the instructions that they have received. The octahedrons organize with a flat-side to flat-side alignment that is based upon positive and negative polarities, like those we find at each end of a battery or a magnet. As the octahedrons align, a reality is formed. That reality is expressed in creation as a form of matter or as an experience. As a whole structure, reality looks a lot like this:

FIGURE 2. THE FABRIC OF CREATION, OUR MAP TO CREATIVE IMAGINING

As you might notice, between the octahedrons are empty spaces. We'll call these the null zones. It is in these spaces that our thoughts, prayers, and intentions travel. As we express a desire of any kind, that expression travels as energy through the null zones. As it does, the octahedrons, which are also energy, receive the messages. As the messages are received, the octahedrons begin to wobble and then rearrange themselves by rolling in place, thus reharmonizing and creating a different reality.

We Talk to Creation, and It Talks Back

How we communicate our wants and desires into the creative process has everything to do with the outcome. Most of the time, when we mean to create a new experience or event in our lives, we do so with concerns, worries, and even fear. We make each outcome dependent upon other things, such as someone else doing their part. Basically, we create with an entire set of what ifs.

Without necessarily meaning to, we often precondition our wishes using subconscious input, such as our fears. Maybe we don't feel like we deserve what we want. Maybe we feel that someone else has to participate for our wishes to come true. Maybe we . . . ? The possible reasons we sabotage our creative process are unlimited.

We also repeat our requests over and over again, wishing, hoping, wanting, even needing. And yet things don't quite work out. Part of the reason is that we are focused on the process and not the outcome.

If we focus on the process, what we are communicating to Creation is that we don't believe in the truth of what we want. We become shortsighted to the point of not envisioning the outcome, just the process, and therefore there is no outcome!

Do you use affirmations to create life events or what you want? Affirmations are statements that we say over and over again so that we can continue to believe in and be reminded of a specific outcome. Yes? Well, never, never, never, ever, *ever* use them again.

Affirmations create dependence. Affirmations are crutches that maintain our sense of need.

Each moment that we exist, we are literally different from the way we were only a moment before. We are constantly reharmonizing ourselves to our environments, other people, everything. (Typically, when our children are small, they naturally reharmonize. As they get older and begin to feel the pressures of society, their friends, and changing values and perspectives, they begin to fight the natural course by becoming more and more individualized, hence closing off their innate gifts.)

When we make a statement in one moment, we do so with a specific set of energetic harmonics. When we repeat ourselves later, we are harmonically different, so our request is communicated differently as well. Not only are we harmonically different, but our thoughts and feelings are also changing in every moment.

When we repeat ourselves with a different set of thoughts and feelings, we change the original message and confuse the creative process. Instead of the particulates changing position to create the reality we wanted, they wobble in place without rearranging, and we receive little to no benefit from our intentions. Or worse, we get chaos that looks like we might get what we want, but the possibility fizzles out and never fully happens. The chaos happens, but we never really get to the outcome. Little do we know that the fizzle was our own doing! Sending mixed messages to the universal creative process looks a lot like figure 3.

Communicating Messages for Success

How we present our desires to the creative process is a big deal. If we are *asking,* what we want only *might* happen or we *may* succeed. Asking also means that something or someone outside of us is responsible for the change we want.

> *Nothing and no one outside of us gives us our experiences. Only we give our experiences to ourselves.*

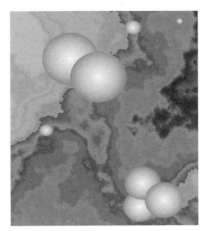

FIGURE 3. INTENT WITH DOUBT OR FEAR—A SORRY STATE OF AFFAIRS!
THE MESSAGE THAT COULD HAVE BEEN PURE BECOMES FRAGMENTED
WHEN ACCOMPANIED BY OUR FEARS AND DOUBTS.

Asking is a subservient attitude. To ask denies not only our power of creation but our ability to act as Creator on our own behalf. Remember that we are whole and perfect beings of Creation. Having the kinds of experiences we want is our birthright. We have free will and the ability to imagine infinite kinds of realities. We are the creator that we seek. Therefore, we don't ask—we command. The key is:

That which we seek also seeks us.
Anything that we desire is already available to us. By
virtue of the fact that we desire it at all, our desire is
already a reality.

But if we don't believe in our creative process, then what we want will never be so. We must believe, without a doubt, completely and fully, in everything that we intend to create—and then let it go.

Right about now you are probably wondering, "What does she mean, let it go?" Sending a prayer or intention into the universal process to create a reality is a lot like throwing a ball. We imagine how we will feel when we have arrived in our new experience, filled with the passion of experiencing it with no doubt or fear, and then we *let it go.*

Or look at it this way: Imagine having your intention in your hand. It is real, it is alive, and it is of your desire. That intention is the impetus for your new reality. It is the fuel for the fire, the water for the drought. To allow your intention to grow, it needs to be fed, just like all other living things. The kind of nourishment it requires is passion.

Passion of the heart is the fuel of all Creation.

We have to pray *and* move our feet. How true it is! As we send our command outward into the infinite, we must believe and know without a doubt that it is already so. We must know that we have created a reality, and now we must do our part to meet that reality at the moment in time when it intersects with our current path. As that intersection occurs, we have our new reality exactly or better than we had imagined.

The real key here is not to have expectations.

What? No expectations?

No.

None.

The reason is:

When we have expectations, we set ourselves up for a pass-or-fail situation. We get exactly what we expected or less. Nothing more. If we do not set parameters on our expectations, we are allowing any number of infinite possibilities to come together for a reality even greater that we could have imagined!

I will tell you a great story. Years ago when I left my hometown to marry my husband, I gave away my car to someone who needed it. I wasn't going to need one for a while. Several years after that, I was very sick and not able to work for a long period of time. In the meantime, my husband was transferred to another state nearly three thousand miles away.

After we moved and I began to heal and become strong again, I began to feel trapped without a car. I had enough money in the bank for an old used vehicle, but that was about it. I had just started working again and wasn't sure what monthly car payment I could afford or if I could afford any at all. I also travel extensively with my work, and my trips often include driving to out-of-town venues. I needed a vehicle that I could depend upon, so that as I traveled alone I would know I was safe.

I began to search the Internet for cars for sale in my general vicinity. It was a tedious process, to say the least. I was sitting at my computer screen, exasperated, when I heard "Go to the Lexus dealer!" I doubted my guidance, thinking, "Oh, yeah, right! Like I even have enough money to talk with those Lexus salespeople, let alone buy a car from them." (But a Lexus *was* the car I had secretly wanted for years!)

And then another thought crossed my mind: "Well, they probably do get great quality trade-ins. Maybe they have something affordable."

I imagined how I would feel in my new car, allowed myself to experience the emotions of a successful car-buying experience. I pictured myself sitting in the new car, knowing that everything I wanted or needed was there. I saw myself driving comfortably. Basically, I had left my options open by not defining the outcome too specifically, just with emotions that were positive. I sent a general message, leaving open whatever possibilities might come together to bring the outcome I desired or perhaps something even better.

My husband had promised to take me out to find a vehicle on Saturday. My highly anticipated day came around, and we got in the car to go to town. The conversation went something like this:

"So where do you want to go?"

"Take me to the Lexus dealer, please."

"*What?*" (His eyes were twinkling. By then, he knew me.)

"Yes, please, take me to the Lexus dealer. I heard I could get a great deal there." I didn't tell him who told me—just that I had heard it. (Giggle!)

We arrived at the dealer and met a great salesman. I was honest with the guy from the word go. "Look, I may not be your biggest sale of the day, but if you treat me right, within two years I will be back and that next sale will be well worth your while!" No response. He wasn't impressed. But he did show me three awesome possibilities.

That day I got a practically new car with everything—and I mean *everything*—that I could have dreamed. It was as if I had actually ordered the car I wanted. The car I bought wasn't a Lexus, but it was fantastic. It was only a year old and had few miles, a leather interior, and all of the bells and whistles you can imagine. It even still smelled new.

Apparently there were so many auto dealers in the area that every Saturday the Lexus dealership ran an ad showing one or two cars priced under book value as an incentive to potential buyers to go to the dealer. I was lucky enough to get there early and buy that incentive car! Not only that, but two years later I *was* back to upgrade to my new Lexus. I believed it with all my heart that I would go back for a Lexus, and my intention became reality!

When we send a clear message out to Creation, we get a clear response—a successful manifestation of the reality we meant to create.

Contrary to the mixed creative message depicted in figure 3, figure 4 displays how a clear and solid intention, communicated with strength and power, creates our new reality:

Faith has everything to do with our creative power. Faith is nothing more than a solid belief in something that we can't see or understand. If we want to be successful in our creative endeavors, we must believe fully and completely that what we have intended is done!

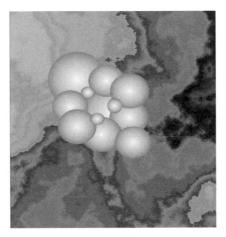

FIGURE 4. INTENT WITH PASSION: COHESIVE
COMMUNICATION WITHOUT A DOUBT!

One of the words that comes up a lot when I work with clients is "abundance." Abundance means:

1. **Large amount** A more than plentiful quantity of something

2. **Affluence** A lifestyle with more than adequate material provisions

3. **Fullness** A fullness of Spirit that overflows

And yet I hear this word most often when it is spoken by people who don't value themselves. The concept of abundance has escaped them on every personal level. To them, abundance is something that comes from outside of them. They are self-perceived victims to a world that doesn't give them what they want. They want, they need, and yet they don't value themselves to any degree. Self-criticism is their norm; they beat themselves up for what they haven't done, had, or accomplished. Many appear defeated. The truth is:

*Abundance is value, period. Money is value. Even joy is value. We are value. **How can we attract value when we don't value ourselves?***

Get What You Give

The first thing that has to happen if we are going to have what we want is that we have to know *without a doubt* that *we deserve anything and everything* that we want. To do this means that we must accept not only the possibility that we are perfection, but also the reality that we are, beyond a shadow of a doubt, the most miraculous creature in all Creation.

We must be willing to receive as easily as we give.

Most of us give to others quite easily. We give our time, our energy, even our belongings away. But when it comes to receiving, that can be difficult.

If we have trouble receiving, it is because we have not acknowledged our value.

Our sense of personal value is easily reflected in our ability to receive. When we say things like "Aw, you shouldn't have," or "I don't deserve this," or "I can't believe you did this," we are reinforcing our belief that we are less than and not deserving. When we receive something from another person, it also doesn't mean that we owe them. *There is a vast difference between a prearranged honest exchange and someone just doing something nice for you.*

Gratitude

Learning to receive is nothing more than simply knowing that we are worth whatever the circumstance is and learning to be gracefully *grateful*.

When we have gratitude, we open the door to more and greater gifts in our lives.

Gratitude is a gift in itself. When we remember to be grateful, we are saying that yes, we are perfection, and yes, we deserve what we get, and yes, bring more at every opportunity! Gratitude comes in all forms and for all reasons. Here are just a few things for which we can be grateful:

Our lives

Our success

Our challenges

What we have learned

What we still need to know

What we have

What we don't have

What is *now*

Our health

Our families

The love that we give

The love that we receive

Our friends

Our abilities to imagine

Our free will

Our perfection

The list is infinite.

Exercise: Gratitude, Creation, and More Gratitude

First of all, take a deep breath. Think of ten things for which you are grateful. Let that gratitude expand your heart space. Terrific!

Next, think of something that you want or need. Imagine that you have put that thing into your hand. Hold it gently. Imagine how you will feel when you are in the reality of your creation. Next, close your eyes and bring the feelings of gratitude into your hands with your creation. Now throw your creation away from you. Know that as your intention travels farther and farther away, it is actually getting closer and closer to returning to you as a full-blown reality. Relax, breathe, and know without a doubt that your intention is now a reality, that you and it will meet in an exact moment in time. Remember to watch for the signs showing you how you can move toward the coming moment of manifestation, and know that you have already created the reality.

How long does it take for your reality to occur? Sometimes it happens instantaneously; at other times, it takes a little while. Only *you* can determine the outcome. How completely do you believe in your creation?

Exercise with Your Child

One sad observation I've made is that children are very often taught to take, and they do not learn to be grateful, to take time to stop and appreciate what they have received. That is because we don't necessarily teach them to be grateful. When kids don't appreciate, they become wasteful, messy, and in any number of other ways demonstrate that they just don't respect what they have. I don't just mean material objects. I mean, for example, when a parent or another goes way out of their way to do something nice for their child, anything that honors that child above all others in the moment. Our children must realize gratitude in such a way that they become thoughtful and balanced in giving and receiving of themselves, others, and everything in between.

With your child, you can do the above exercise in smaller parts. For instance, ask them to name five things for which they are grateful. If they come up with five very quickly, ask them to keep going and name five more.

Ask your child when they were grateful and didn't acknowledge their gratitude appropriately or at all. Let them tell you.

After your child has become more aware of when gratitude is appropriate, reverse the exercise. Ask your child to come up with ideas about how they can give to others instead of receiving. How can they share their efforts, talents, or whatever?

Remind them that it is just as important to be grateful for the opportunity to give as it is to be grateful for being on the receiving end. The idea is for them to learn that giving and receiving is a cycle—not a tit for tat, but a constancy of flow. Explain to your child that giving and receiving are part of the natural rhythm of life and that in order to maintain balance they must learn to do both equally as well.

14

EMBRACE YOUR GIFTS

And celebrate your children's!

The main reason that we often begin to feel as if we don't fit or don't belong is because of our inner gifts—our sensitivities, intuition, awareness, and abilities to express honestly and completely what is in our hearts and minds at any given moment.

Some of us have always had a great sense of being different, that we just don't fit in the scope of humanity. We feel as if we need to be somewhere else or even to "go home." But where is that? Some of us began having otherworldly visions or intuitive knowledge as far back as we can remember. But then our parents and others told us that those things weren't real, and we began to feel set aside, hiding our encounters. Sometimes we feel things so deeply that nothing in our language could express the profundity of what we experience.

No matter what we have gone through or continue to, all of the incidents reflect the gifts that we have inside of us. These gifts can become excellent tools for a greater life experience, or we can choose to become victims of them. Worse, we can propagate in our children the feelings of being alone and set aside.

The Children of Now are even more sensitive than we were. They have the innate ability to absorb, with their entire being, everything that is happening around them. Their bodies are like antennae, picking up every nuance in their environment. They come to us with stories that seem to be too strange or unbelievable to comprehend, and we tell them that the spirit they are talking to isn't real. Or that they really aren't seeing angels. Or that only doctors can heal people. Or that they can't possibly know the things they tell us, so they must have learned or heard those things somewhere.

Out of ignorance, we do to our children exactly what was done to us: deny their experiences and abilities outright. It is time to wake up to the fact that we are, each and all, filled with abilities and gifts that don't make much sense, yet we know and feel things that on some level of reality are very real.

Most of us have had some sort of out-of-the-ordinary experiences that made us wonder or, worse, that made us afraid because we didn't understand what was happening. We all have the innate ability to look, see, hear, and feel beyond what we understand and into the realms of the infinite. Just because we had experiences doesn't mean that we are weird or set aside. Instead, our experiences confirm that yes,

we are part of a greater whole.

And that is just fine.

Our Gifts Are Tools for Life

So what if your dead grandmother comes to you in your dreams? Did she have a message for you? *So what* if you knew something before it happened? Did you follow your intuition and avoid disaster? *Who cares* if you hear someone talking to you about things you don't know about? What if the information is good and helps you? *What if* your intuition was right, and what you thought you knew was, in fact, *really true?* Is saying "I knew it!" enough, or is there something greater happening? Stop holding your breath and thinking that all of a sudden you are more divine or talented than other human beings. You aren't. We all have the ability to have these experiences. The question is, do we use it? The truth is that you are simply becoming who you have always been. More to the point, you are remembering how to use your innate abilities. These are gifts that are simply part of who you are. In fact,

There are things beyond our understanding that are all real—and that is OK. There is nothing to fear!

Honest!

Our sensitivities can actually help guide us in our lives. A gut reaction to something is a gift. That reaction is telling us to pay attention. Danger! Danger! Look past the illusion and *see!* But do we listen? Our bodies tell us more than we can imagine. At the first sign of a situation that is out of bounds with our inner truth, our bodies tense, usually either in the chest or abdomen. We hold our breath for a moment. And then, well, we either listen to our bodies or ignore them and plunge right into a situation that ultimately isn't a good thing.

Our internal gifts help us to see whether we are on the right track or straying into dangerous territory. Our intuition doesn't just happen once in a while. It is there all of the time, prodding us to pay attention, but often we ignore its message as a crazy thought or a passing erroneous piece of information. Only later, of course, do we find out that we were right on in the first place!

Our human habit of mentally processing everything is part of our survival mechanism and keeps our intuition at bay. Thinking sets up an entire set of nerve-firing patterns in our brains, and that pattern locks the doors to our higher knowing. When we defend ourselves by being "rational," thinking about things over and over again, the truth is lost, and we step into directions that aren't necessarily good for us.

Being present in the now really helps. By that I mean not looking outward in anticipation or concern about what will happen later, or looking into the past to try and understand what the heck happened. Have all of our attention right here, right now.

It isn't as easy as we think. *But* if we allow our innate gifts to come forward, we have all of the discernment we need and all of the awareness necessary to make great decisions or to just go with the flow.

Being in the now and letting our natural abilities guide us is pure freedom to the nth degree. We can relax into the now without worry or concern and begin to notice all of the opportunities that come our way. We become free of our self-imposed chains and are able to live freely.

Living in the now is the ultimate definition of faith. When we are able to simply trust that we are perfect and doing the perfect thing in every moment, magic happens.

Magic is everywhere! The only question is, are we noticing?

We Are Sacred Beings

When we begin to notice the magic, we begin to see the little clues in every now that direct us, connect us, guide us to the most exquisite choices that open our lives into fullness and completeness. We begin to operate from our sacred selves. After all, we are created of all that is holy.

Now I don't mean holy in a religious sense. Religion allows only saints and prophets, priests, and other singularly identified people to carry the description of holy.

*What I am talking about is recognizing that **we are sacred beings** who are created from all that is divine and are therefore operating as aspects of the divine.*

One of my favorite definitions for the word *sacred* (taken from *dictionary.net*): "Designated or exalted by a divine sanction; possessing the highest title to obedience, honor, reverence, or veneration; entitled to extreme reverence; venerable."

We are that: sacred in every sense of the word. It is only our perspectives that warp our sense of the sacred in ourselves and others. Since we are created of the divine, we can consider ourselves sanctioned. And if we are divinely sanctioned, we can be or do anything that we can imagine.

Even if we have not recognized our inner perfection, we remain constructed of particles of the infinite that have manifested as matter and become animated into the form of human being. There is no escaping our origin. We are living representations of the divine. Therefore, each of us is sacred.

We are all holy. We all have the innate and indelible right to be who we are, with our free will and immense gifts, to create a life that is fully abundant and exuberant!

So what are we waiting for? Let's drop the pretense that we are anything less than perfect and get on with living from a sense of sacred perfection.

Whatever glimpses we may have had beyond the reality that we describe as normal are simply reminders that there is much more than we currently remember. There is so much potential in what we don't know. Just relax into your experiences and remember that it is all perfection!

Exercise: Returning to the Divine Perspective

Think of yourself as a divine being. What is your first reaction? Disbelief? Do you want to laugh? Do you feel that this can't be true because you are so imperfect?

Look again. Look deeper. Close your eyes. Breathe. Ask yourself to reveal the hidden you. Keep breathing. Let your breath rise into your heart, opening it slowly until you feel as if you will burst. You won't.

Send your attention into your full heart. Breathe in the feeling of fullness. How does that feel? Keep doing it. Allow yourself to float freely in your heart space for as long as you desire. In this state, you have returned to the divine. Breathe this feeling throughout your body until you feel intensely light in every cell and accept that whoever you are, whatever you do, you are a whole and perfect child of Creation and nothing or no one can ever change that but you. And even then, the only thing you can really change is your perception.

Exercise with Your Child

What is it that your child believes about themselves that begins the pattern of feeling separate from others? Have you noticed? Is it issues of confidence or thinking they are a dork or weird or something equally imperfect? Address these perceptions with your child from the standpoint that they are whole and perfect beings and that these kinds of thoughts and feelings are self-effacing and not truth.

Take your child through the meditation described in the previous exercise for adults. Use terminology they can relate to. Teach your child how to breathe into their heart space, and instruct them to do this whenever they begin to feel any kind of negative self-image.

15

WHOSE CHILDREN ARE THEY, ANYWAY?

Don't let the bullies get you down!

How many times have well-meaning people tried to tell us how to raise our children, judged us based on what our children have done or said, or dictated to us what we had to do with our children?

This kind of thing has to stop right now.

Our children are *our* children. If we have brought them into this world, adopted them, or come into the care of them by whatever set of circumstances, they are our children. It is not anyone else's job to raise them. It is ours, plain and simple. Sometimes we believe so strongly that our children reflect who we are that we don't step up to other people and say our truth because we are embarrassed. Sometimes we feel so insignificant that when our children need us to be in our power, we just don't know how. Hopefully by the time you have reached this page, you will have begun to find at least a glimpse of the magnificent creature that you are.

Sometimes when our children begin to exercise their free will, acting in ways that are in conflict with what we want for them, we don't have the time or the energy or the courage to tell them that their behavior is not acceptable. Sometimes it is just easier to let it go for now. Unfortunately, all of those little nows can add up to one overbearing, spoiled, and dysfunctional child who has no boundaries or social skills.

If we are going to take on the responsibility of raising any child, no matter how they came to be with us, we must truly take their care to heart. No one else is going to care about our kids like we do. No one else is going to have the same set of values that we do, and no one else has any business telling us how to raise our children. Sometimes they are just plain wrong.

I remember as a young single mother being called in to talk with my son's fourth-grade teacher. Her summons was ominous, and I was quite intimidated by it. After the initial pleasantries had been exchanged, the teacher slid a piece of paper across her desk to me. Her expression told me that whatever was on that paper was vile and horrid. I looked at the paper and saw that, over and over again, all over the paper, my son had drawn what the teacher had interpreted to be male genitalia. God! The drawings did look like that, sort of. I thought, "Now what do I say? This is embarrassing!"

Well, I assured the teacher that I would handle the situation and that it wouldn't happen again. I went home madder than hell, not because my son had drawn these things, but because he had placed *me* in a position of total embarrassment. I was out for blood.

When I started to talk with my son about it (the teacher had kept the paper, so I had to describe what I had seen), he said, "Oh, you mean the skull and crossbones? Yeah, I was practicing drawing them, but I couldn't get it right." Oh, God. Because his teacher, a person in the position of authority, had told me my son had been wrong, I had believed her. This was not OK! I started to laugh long and hard, and so did my son when I told him what his teacher had thought. We alternated from hysterical laughter to shock and awe that she could have thought such a thing. Her interpretation said a lot about her! Fortunately, I had approached the situation by giving my son a chance to explain his side of it. And at a later date I did make a point of telling the teacher what my son had really drawn!

Too often we leap to please others, to conform to social rules and mores, before we know the whole story.

We are so ingrained to follow the rules and do what is right by someone else's standards that we often forget what is right for us.

Worse, we turn our heads and do nothing. We let someone else deal with it. We let other people deal with our children the way we should have. Unfortunately they don't necessarily do what we would have done or even approved of.

Conversely, other people take the position that they have the right to dictate what is best for our children. More and more I am hearing stories from parents, particularly single mothers, that their child's school is threatening serious action if they don't do with their child what the school wants. In many cases, the schools are demanding that the parents put their children on drugs. In fact, since my international bestseller *The Children of Now* came out, I have had no fewer than a half dozen parents contact me with similar stories. They all say that, for whatever reason, their child's school had deemed that the child needed to be drugged, and when they refused, Social Services showed up at their door and threatened to take the child away if the child wasn't drugged. God!

This is an extreme example, but one that is valid and happening even as we speak. Our society has an archaic view of how to raise our children. Our kids are not like we were. Many of them are highly aware creatures who absorb everything happening around them. Because of the intensity of what they feel, they don't sit still. They don't know this sensitivity isn't "normal." They are just being who they are. If our society and our school systems would revamp the rules, the classrooms, and the social expectations and generally relax about our children, we wouldn't have the problems we have.

Truly it is up to us to stand up and be counted in the name of the children we have created.

This goes for any circumstance. We must give our kids good, solid guidelines, values, discipline, and frameworks in order for them to learn to live in our world, but we also have to give them the freedom to not only explore, but also to become who they are. As it stands, societal demands do not allow adults, let alone our children, the freedom of expression!

The only way to change this situation is for us to take a stand and say no to the unrealistic expectations of a society that has obviously run amuck as a whole anyway. Good, honoring social values are hard to find beneath all of the media hype that says that social values are what we wear and that what we have makes us who we are.

We are who we are, as are our children, in spite of external influences.

A great deal of the problem lies in the fact that many of us, as soon as our children are home or shortly after, put them in a little seat in front of the TV, or we farm them out to someone else until it is convenient for us to pick them up. We involve them in every activity in creation in the name of expanding their horizons when often what we are really doing is avoiding having to be with them ourselves.

Our kids are then not nurtured; they are socialized into having to be way too responsible way too soon and in such a way that they mature socially beyond their years. The rest of the problem is that they may have matured socially, but not emotionally and certainly not physically. We end up with socially mature kids who have no idea how to process their feelings. They become inured to the feelings of others and give in to the peer pressure to ridicule others and engage in other irresponsible behaviors.

It is certainly understandable that some children have to go to latch-key programs or other after-school care. It takes a lot of hours of work for families to keep up these days. And once in a while parents need a little time-out.

But the truth is that we need to spend time with our children. Left to society, they will become insensitive, unsatisfied human beings who would rather live in the fantasy world of video games and movies, who have highly inflated self-images or, worse, antisocial behaviors. Our children need us. They need to be nurtured, not street smart. They need to know who they are and where they came from. They need tradition and a predictable framework in order to develop in a healthy way physically, mentally, emotionally, and spiritually. They need to know they are loved, and it is up to us to show them.

You may feel that these are harsh words. If so, it is for one of two reasons. Either you are loving and nurturing your child and giving them every benefit of good parenting, or at least the best you know how, or you are exactly whom I am talking about and having a moment of denial. If you are the latter, keep breathing and ask yourself what you needed as a kid that you very likely didn't get. Then see if you are still feeling the same way. The reason that we adults have so many issues is that those issues weren't addressed for us when we were kids. And they weren't addressed because no one knew how to do so. These are different times.

Since the release of *The Children of Now*, I have been exposed to huge numbers of stories, from every aspect of society and from parents and caregivers, about what is happening with our children today. The gamut of situations is mind-boggling. The common thread in all the stories says that society needs to catch up. It is not 1863; it is the twenty-first century.

And we need to have the courage to speak on behalf of our children. We can't wait for others in authority to do anything. We *are* the authority when it comes to our children.

Many parents are homeschooling their children in a valiant effort to make a change. Homeschooling is a great way to go if you know what you are doing and you can consistently maintain the momentum for your child. I have been in some homes where purportedly homeschooled kids were watching TV all day and there was never a lesson to be seen. There is also now a grassroots movement to open pilot schools that cater to the needs of our kids. There are day and summer camps that provide good, healthy environments and values for them. Springing up in the least expected places are activities that further the sensitivities of our children and have a focus on social consciousness. There are countless ways that we can support our children outside of the norm, and yet simply supporting our children is about as normal as it gets.

However you choose to be a parent to your children, do so responsibly, with love, and don't be afraid to stand up for them. They are not a reflection of whether or not you did a good job. They are the future of our planet, the propagation of the human race. What kinds of values will they take into tomorrow or leave behind today?

Parenting from Your New Perspective

Here are a few keys for parenting from your newly learned perspectives:

- Give them your heart and soul, no matter what.

- Teach them to be kind and considerate human beings, free of prejudice or judgment.

- Give them what they need, not your problems.

- Know them inside and out, and be in tune with changes in their countenance. Those changes could signal things you and they need to talk about.

- Give them a framework to live by. Good structure allows a child to have a feeling of safety.

- Live equally with them. Let them know that they matter and that you don't consider them less than anyone else.

- Be present for them, now, in this moment.

- Communicate freely with your children, undefended and with honesty. Listen to them. Hear their words, because often, in their innocence, they are wise beyond their years.

- Give them not your stress, but the mysteries you behold in life.

- Talk gently with your children. Do not be so quick to admonish them that you miss the truth of what really happened.

- Consider what each request from your child means to them, even when it isn't important to you.

- Say no and mean it when you must, but don't be so ready to say no that you forget how to say yes.

- Consider that whatever you teach them, no matter how you do it, your message has been conveyed, your child has learned its meaning, and that message is now part of your child's belief system. Once you have conveyed your message, there is no turning back.

- Live with your children as if there is no tomorrow and yesterday no longer matters.

- Be honest, even if it embarrasses you. Your child needs the truth, not convenient answers.

- Have joy; find reasons to laugh, even in the darkest moments.

- Share not your expectations of your children, but your pride that they tried at all.

- Let them be who they are, no matter what, even when you wish they would be something else. And if you do wish that, keep your opinions to yourself.

- Be interested even when you are tired.

- Be strong for them, a living example of life's possibilities.

- Teach your child not to be afraid, but instead to enter each unknown with excitement for what it may have to offer.

- Be an example of the endless possibilities that life has to offer them.

- And most of all, love them with all that you are and all that ever was. They are children of the One, as are you, and you are both perfection.

How you raise your child, and the person your child becomes is entirely up to you. You know what to do. Don't be afraid to step up to the plate.

16

THE ART OF PARENTING AS A WELL-BALANCED, WHOLE AND PERFECT, MAGNIFICENT HUMAN BEING

Or the freedom of no longer needing to guard
your every move because you know who you
are, and that's all that matters!

A journey through the heart and soul brings us revelations and re-
alizations about behaviors and issues we didn't know we had. We
begin to find freedom, first from our own binding perceptions and
then from the perceptions of others, as we learn to eject our old
tapes and learn new patterns of behavior. We begin to understand
just how complex our defense systems have become.

The truth is that everything is *is simple.*

Life. Every bit of it.

When we understand just how tightly bound we have become
simply by doing or being the "right thing," we are likely to be as-
tounded. We realize that we had lost our way and were on a nebulous

path to Never-Never Land via Mr. Toad's Wild Ride. And we were taking our kids with us.

If you do nothing else, take the tools in this book and work with them. None of them are too hard, and all of them are beneficial for changing your life into anything and everything that you can imagine. When your children see that you are happy, relaxed, undefended, truthful, and everything else we have addressed here, they become those things too.

We have learned to accept ourselves just as we are, knowing that who and what we are is the truth and everything that anyone has told us beyond that is an illusion created to maintain superiority. We are perfection in spite of what anyone else thinks. When we are perfection, our children feel the same way. They are less afraid of being substandard in our eyes.

We have looked at how telling the truth sets us free, and that while being truthful takes a little practice, when we are, we no longer have to cover our tracks or feel insignificant. Honest communication with our children is paramount to healthy relationships, as well as their ability to learn how to discern what truth is to them. Their ability to know the truth is innate. We are the ones who teach them how to forget and begin to live untruths. Let the truth ring out loud and clear, with passion and compassion in your heart and the hearts of your children, so that they learn to be unafraid of the lies of others.

We have realized that our fears often run our entire lives, and we have learned how to identify those fears, owning them so that finally we can let them go. Help your children recognize their inner fears and make it OK to talk about those fears, so that your children are less stressed and can become confident in themselves.

Our passion had eluded many of us, but we have realized that passion is a multitude of things and at the bottom of all of those possibilities is a heart open to whatever we experience. Encourage your children's exuberance, even when you feel it is silly. Let them realize that self-expression is honest communication and not something to hide away.

We have learned that it is fine to question everything and that asking questions relieves the tension of holding in our fear of what we don't understand. Encourage your children to ask thoughtful, intentional questions and to, in turn, listen to the answers they receive. Support them in having their own opinions and in knowing that whether anyone else agrees or disagrees isn't important.

Together we have come to the realization that we can finally stop fixing ourselves, that all of the self-help in the world isn't going to help anything if we don't truly grasp its meaning and apply it to our life experiences. We have learned how to identify within ourselves that which we need to know for our own perspectives and to make more positive decisions. Let your children know that no matter what anyone else says or does, those actions are based solely on opinions—theirs—and do not need to cause injury or loss of confidence within your children.

We have studied all of the reasons we don't need to fear change and why the result of change is magnificence. We now know why we should let the flow carry us into the unknown, filled with excitement at the prospect of the infinite possibilities that are available to us when we just let ourselves go. We know that we don't have to resist, only be in the now, for now is all there ever is. Encourage your children to create some kind of change every day in their lives, to step off of the pinnacle into the unknown with excitement as they consider the infinite possibilities that are open to them because of those changes.

We have learned that we can have it all, and we can laugh the entire way through our life journeys. Remind your children to look up and into the eyes of others and to have a sense of humor about what they see. Remind them that they can create whatever they want in life, that whatever they have imagined must be so.

Perhaps we are now more aware of how we interact in all of the relationships in our lives. Maybe, just maybe, we can begin to recognize the dynamics at play around us as others act out their stories. Give your children the example of whole and healthy relationships that are filled with joy. Leave behind the idea that anyone can fill any part of you, and teach your children of this fullness.

And speaking of stories, we have become aware of how we create our inner stories to keep us from truths that we don't want to see. We know now that those truths are far greater than the deceit that causes us ongoing pain. Teach your children to tell themselves the truth even when it hurts. They will be far greater people for having learned the power of the truth and, with their recognition of and comfort with the truth, your children will know others much more thoroughly as well.

Our gifts are part of who we are, just as are our children's gifts are part of who they are, and these gifts should be embraced and honored as part of the sacred in each of us. Children who display a wide variety of gifts have been gracing our world since the 1980s, when the Indigo kids first came along. Now, with the Crystalline Children, Star Kids, Transitional Children, and the new wave of Children of Now just beginning to appear, with their energy fields of complete white energy, we have a lot to do.

All children are very, very special. Different is fabulous, no matter how it looks. Don't turn away or be frightened by what you don't understand. Stand up and celebrate every child every day.

Our children are ours to raise, and what anyone else thinks, says, or does are subject to our discernment and approval. Remember this always, and stand up for your kid first, regardless of who thinks what about how they should be raised.

Lighten up with your children and yourself. Remember that there is no secret. We can have whatever we want. And we want a lot for ourselves and for our children. What we give them will be with them as the framework for their entire lives. Think about that: their entire lives.

Parting Words

Recently, during a trip to Scotland, I took a group on a journey of sacred sites. As we were standing in the midst of one of the stone henges, I had a most profound revelation. The group waited for me to say something wise and spiritual. What came out of my mouth was a surprise to everyone there, including me. As I talked, their eyes got big, and they started to fidget. At one point, there was a nearly audible gasp as the recognition of my words sank in. Good. I was hitting home. Perfect.

It went something like this:

Look around you. This is a place that is considered to be sacred. As each of you entered this place, you felt that it was giving something to you. You began to feel the holiness here. You became reverent as soon as you walked through that gate. Many of you began to have spiritual experiences and felt your hearts expanding. I could feel you feeling the depths of your experiences.

But it isn't about this place.

It is about you. Life is sacred. **You are sacred.**

What you are feeling is coming from within you. It is based upon your perceptions, your emotions, your hopes, wishes, and dreams. And you are only allowing yourselves to feel this in a place that you feel is appropriate or safe.

Let yourselves feel this in every moment of life. Feel deeply. Live fully.

I have a question for you. Don't answer it for me, or us, just answer it for you.

*The ancients left this place for people to come and visit millennia after they were here. They knew the importance of tradition and ritual, of what is sacred. What will you leave upon this earth when **you** are gone? What have you given in return for what you have received? Or are you all just taking what you can, while you can?* (Gasp!)

Know that for every action there is a reaction, a rippling outward of consequences that continue on infinitely.

Know that every action that you take, every word that you speak, every thought that you have, any energy of any kind that you expend, affects the entirety. And you are affected by all that happens within the entirety. This is a mutual exchange that happens on the most minute as well as on the grandest levels of being.

Live intentionally. Know that whatever you choose in any given moment is the most perfect decision you could have ever made simply because you made it.

That you have the free will to determine the outcome of any situation in your life is a gift from the heavens that will never wear out.

*Receiving and taking are two completely different animals. To take denotes possession. To receive denotes a gift. Let everything that you experience be a gift. Receive gracefully and with gratitude, and always, always be willing to do your part. You have to pray **and** move your feet.*

And remember that all of your actions in all of your life leave an indelible mark upon this world and beyond.

To this I would only add:

That indelible mark, everything that you create now, will be lived through your children and your children's children and their children and their children's children.

We have the power to change the world today, as well as our future world, through the actions and patterns, beliefs and perceptions, that we hand down as our legacy to the Children of Now.

And they are listening not only with their ears and other earthly senses. They are absorbing everything around them like sponges, missing nothing.

We must be vigilant.

First with ourselves.

Then with our Children.

As we are, we exercise the very power of the infinite right here on earth and fuel it for all time.

About the Author

Meg Blackburn Losey, PhD, is the author of the international best-seller *The Children of Now* and *Conversations with the Children of Now.* Her internet radio show, "Continuum," is broadcast on *ShirleyMacLaine.com* the first and third Wednesdays of every month.

Dr. Meg has recently served as a consultant to *Good Morning America* and *20/20* News. Her expertise on issues relating to children of the consciousness evolution is greatly in demand.

Dr. Meg is a Master Healer, speaker, and teacher. She is an ordained minister in both Spiritual Science and Metaphysics. She is a PhD of Holistic Life Coaching and holds a doctoral degree in Metaphysics. She is a medical intuitive and the developer of the Seventh Sense Attunement® healing process.

Visit her at *www.spiritlite.com.*

To Our Readers